The Melchizedek Priesthood Robes

Generation Zion, Volume 3

Dennis Grimes

Published by Dennis Grimes, 2024.

While every precaution has been taken in the preparation of this book, the publisher assumes no responsibility for errors or omissions, or for damages resulting from the use of the information contained herein.

THE MELCHIZEDEK PRIESTHOOD ROBES

First edition. March 28, 2024.

Copyright © 2024 Dennis Grimes.

ISBN: 979-8224667451

Written by Dennis Grimes.

Table of Contents

This book is dedicated first to my Heavenly Father, my Lord Jesus Christ, the Anointed One of Israel, and the Holy Spirit.

I would also like to dedicate this book to my family, who gave me the time to study, pray, and seek God's direction for the writing of this book.

COPYRIGHT

Scripture quotations marked (NKJV) are taken from the NEW KING JAMES VERSION®. Copyright© 1982 by Thomas Nelson, Inc. Used by permission. All rights reserved.

Scripture taken from The Orthodox Jewish Bible Copyright © 2011 by AFI International. All rights reserved.

Scripture quotations marked (NLT) are taken from the *Holy Bible*, New Living Translation, copyright ©1996, 2004, 2015 by Tyndale House Foundation. Used by permission of Tyndale House Publishers, Carol Stream, Illinois 60188. All rights reserved.

Scripture quotations are from Revised Standard Version of the Bible, copyright © 1946, 1952, and 1971 National Council of the Churches of Christ in the United States of America. Used by permission. All rights reserved worldwide.

Scripture taken from The Expanded Bible. Copyright ©2011 by Thomas Nelson. Used by permission. All rights reserved.

Scripture quotations marked (TLB) are taken from *The Living Bible*, copyright © 1971 by Tyndale House Foundation. Used by permission of Tyndale House Publishers, Carol Stream, Illinois 60188. All rights reserved.

PREFACE

KEEPER OF THE WARDROBE

According to 2 Kings 22:14 and 2 Chronicles 34:22 there was a "keeper of the wardrobe" for the priestly garments. The garments were to remain undefiled because the priests at that time had defiled them by burning incense to other gods (demons and fallen angels). This keeper was Huldah the prophetess. Her husband was a Levitical priest. She represents the prophetic Bride and the prophets that keep the wardrobe of the priests pure and undefiled. Because Jesus is the High Priest of the Melchizedek priesthood, and we are His Bride and priests. As part of the prophets and prophetic people, in the name of Jesus, release the garments of the priests to be put on/(en dü o).

Purpose of the Remaining Garments

In the Epistle of the Revelation of Jesus Christ chapter 2, versus 18-29, Jesus declares the spirit of Jezebel has corrupted the church of Thyatira. Through the progression of each aspect of putting on the robes, humility, and the turban of justice with the crown of holiness gives you a new battle technique against the spirit of Jezebel and the whole satanic/demonic kingdom. For this is the harlot church spoken of in Revelation 17. This spirit and those that are associated with it are part of the beast, Queen of Heaven, and anti-Christ system. The Jezebel spirit is an exalting spirit that is determined to rub out the true Church, the "Man Child of God". Also known to us as the "Christ" of Jesus here on Earth according to a different interpretation of Revelation 12. Just to remind you, that this "Christ" is the body of Jesus that helps put down the counterfeit spirits that exalt themselves above Jesus and His Father, who blasphemy the Holy Spirit.

As His Body, we will overcome Jezebel. Let us investigate the remaining garments of the Warrior Priesthood. Every part of the garments are aspects of Jesus Christ that He wants to wrap around you so that you are more clothed or arrayed in Him.

PART I – THE PRIESTLY FINE LINEN EPHOD AND ROBES

Chapter 1: The Fine Linen Ephod Robe

THIS IS THE FIRST TIME when we transition from garments to robes or mantles which is translated the Hebrew word "meh-eel." Meh-eel will be fully discussed about in the *Robe of Righteousness*.

The Ephod Robe

According to Exodus 29:5 (World English Bible (WEB)) the ephod was blue and there was the robe of the ephod. The ephod represents that heaven consumes the priest. This robe is first put on then the robe of righteousness. Note that the linen ephod was only worn only by the High Priest as part of the communication between him and Father God (see Exo. 28:1-4) that was passed down from father to son (see Exo. 29:29) and was made by wise people who had been given the spirit of wisdom.

As it was woven the spirit of wisdom was then imparted and imputed into it from those that weaved it together. These artisans were filled with the spirit of wisdom that God poured out on to them (see Exo. 28:3). The Ephod robe was delegated and given to be used by God as part of the High Priestly vestures that are put on to minister to the Lord and enter His holy presence.

David is seen as wearing an ephod according to 1 Chronicles 15:27. David symbolizes Jesus and the now instituted Melchizedekian priesthood. Because of this change we may also minister to the Lord with the royal ephod put on us. For the colors of the ephod are "of gold, blue, purple, and scarlet *thread,* and fine twined linen" (Exo. 28:6).

The colors have been woven into our spiritual DNA with the nature of God which is symbolized by the gold thread and the blue, purple, and scarlet threads that were originally interwoven into the veil into the Holy of holies. Now that the veil has been torn (see Mat. 27:51; Mar. 15:38; Luke 23:45) between our hearts and minds so should our spirit and soul become aligned and intertwined with our heavenly nature or new man. Our new man supersedes our old man or old nature where it is fully woven with Jesus's nature. This nature should lead us into the heavenly realms, that leads through the torn veil to the royal courtroom of Elohim by which our access is through the blood of the Lamb of God.

The fine line of the Ephod is represented as the righteous acts of the saints (see Rev. 19:8). This type of robe was also put on "the Levites who bore the ark, the singers, and Chenaniah the music master *with* the singers" (1 Chr. 15:27 New King James Version (NKJV)). The ark of the Covenant with the manifest presence of the shekinah glory cloud of Yahweh Elohim now represents us who bear the Covenant of the cross and the resurrection of Jesus to manifest the Holy Spirit who lives in us and wants to be poured out of our hearts in this physical world through the shekinah glory cloud of Yahweh Elohim.

Notice, though not explicitly spoken, Yahweh Elohim was pleased with David for what he did. As previously seen in 2 Samuel 6 that when David was bringing the ark to Jerusalem that Uzzah touched the ark because the oxen had stumbled while being transported and the Yahweh of Hosts became angry and struck Uzzah down and killed him. David was much terrified and afraid of God. For God's presence is holy. We are to treat each other as holy for Yahweh of Hosts is our Commander and Chief. We bear His presence.

As we minister to the Lord with the Ephod, we begin to bear witness that we are before the ark of the New Covenant of Testimony where the Holy Spirit dwells. The Holy Spirit in essence is the visible and invisible presence of Jesus. Jesus is Yahweh of Hosts, who dwells in, on, through, and around us. It is also noteworthy to pray about our position before the ark of the New Covenant that we are to live between the Cherubim where God is also (see 1 Sam. 4:4 New International Version (NIV)).

Priestly Prayer Position

We who are part of the great ark in heaven that are wrapped in earthen vessels love and desire God's manifested presence as much as possible. We want the shekinah glory as much as possible. We are mainly intercessors, prophets, prophetic people, or anyone that prays for God's people that are already part of and yet will be part of God's Kingdom. For this is the Father's heart.

To dwell between the cherubim is a high priestly position. Though we are not the high priest this position is only reserved for Jesus (see Heb. 3:1, 4:14, 6:20). All Christians are called to be priests of the Most High God (see Rev. 1:6). I implore you, as your fellow brother that we continue to keep praying for our country, our leaders for the purpose that God's will be completed for the United States and other nations according to Scripture, God's righteousness comes forth in the Earth, and the nation of Israel, My brethren.

Power of Prayer

When we pray it is with the co-laboring will of the Holy Spirit that changes circumstances in life. We pray with God's mind. To know His mind is to know the Scriptures. The knowledge of the Scriptures allows us to apply the proper Scriptures that the Holy Spirit brings to our mind to help the person we are ministering to. We must minister life to those we encounter and not death. When we pray God's will it is with confidence that we pray and acknowledge that the prayers will be answered by faith which pleases Him (see Mar. 11:24).

Building a Mercy Seat

The more we grow in our character of Jesus, while getting stronger in Him, the better and sharper our prayers will be. The more we build our prayer life, the more we can abide in Him. Our heart is where the Holy of Holies resides. It is here that the mercy seat needs to be built and solidified to house His weighty presence.

God is calling us to build a mercy seat to house His glory. He just does not want a visitation but a habitation for partnership with Him. He wants His presence to linger in a place. Not just a drive by per se or a meet and greet or show and go. He wants us to be able to abide around us in the fulness of who He is.

Do you want this? Can you handle this? Do you need this? If you answered yes, let us go on and see what it takes to build a mercy seat for the Lord. This is where we wear the ephod robe and enter the most holy place and gaze on His face (see Psa. 105:4; Act 7:55). Like Stephen, who was full of the Holy Spirit that he was able to gaze at God the Father, and Jesus Christ. He saw them face to face. Stephen was mystified because of what He saw Abba to be like.

With our Ephod robe on we can enter the presence of our Holy God where we are able to build the mercy seat upon us. This is where we should be able to see ourselves and the One seated between two cherubim. Let's look at like this, the mercy seat was above the Ark of the covenant where it is built on top of your heart. God's glory literally shadows on top of you. It is His magnificent glory that surrounds you. It is up to you to seek this out so that He may speak to you.

The description of the mercy seat as given in Exodus 25:17-22 is given below:

> You shall make a mercy seat of pure gold. Two and a half cubits shall be its length, and a cubit and a half its width. You shall make two cherubim of hammered gold. You shall make them at the two ends of the mercy seat. Make one cherub at the one end, and one cherub at the other end. You shall make the cherubim on its two ends of one piece with the mercy seat. The cherubim shall spread out their wings upward, covering the mercy seat with their wings, with their faces toward one another. The faces of the cherubim shall be toward the mercy seat. You shall put the mercy seat on top

of the ark, and in the ark you shall put the covenant that I will give you. There I will meet with you, and I will tell you from above the mercy seat, from between the two cherubim which are on the ark of the covenant, all that I command you for the children of Israel.

The relationship that we need to build a mercy seat in our lives is that we are continually processing and repenting of sin daily. It is so that we can house God's glory. Jesus had no sin (see 2 Cor. 5:21) in His life and He was able to manifest God's glory when needed according to our Father's will. We live in a fallen body, but when we continue to seek God's face and confess our sins, we can continue living as houses of God's glory. This is where you stand in a position where you are going through a daily process of refinement and processing into pure gold.

The three steps necessary for the Holy Spirit's habitation must engage with is purity of heart, unity of the community, and humility of oneself. To reach the pinnacle of the building of the mercy seat one must be engaged in some form of prayer and worship communion of union with the Holy Spirit. Listening is required for action. When you listen, you are engaged with the mercy seat. This mercy seat is where we lead others to God because we have lived there and know the peace in the presence of God.

Why does YAHWEH choose to dwell between two Cherubim?

Cherubim stand in the presence of God which they are called the "The cherubim of glory" (Luk. 1:19; Heb. 9:5). They proclaim God's holiness and grace which provides salvation and access to the reality of Jesus Christ. This was symbolized in the Old Testament and made a reality in the New Testament.

The Cherubim symbolically look down and see upon the mercy seat with the sprinkled blood which covers the peoples' sins under the Mosaic Law on the Ark of the Covenant. Inside the Ark of the

Covenant there is a golden pot holding the manna, Aaron's rod that budded, and the tablets of the Mosaic covenant (see Heb. 9:4).

We see the position of the cherubim then as being in the presence of God. So again, back to the question "why does Yahweh choose to dwell between two Cherubim?" The truth is based upon the position of the person. The New King James Version renders the italicized word as "between" and the New American Standard Bible renders it as "above." The truth is that word does not exist in the Hebrew. In the Greek Septuagint when compared to the Hebrew the context of the text in those verses are in Psalm 80:1 and Psalm 90:1 is using the words in a form of sitting above the cherubim.

YAHWEH Dwells Between and Above the Two Cherubim

I want to say the truth of the matter should be written in view and position that both renderings are correct. The viewpoint of the word "between" is man looking up to God's throne and knowing that Angels stand guard there. Then showing that the appearance that God dwells "between" the cherubim is correct. The viewpoint of God looking down to mankind is that He dwells "above" the cherubim.

From personal experience when God shows up you know it. You cannot do anything but know that He is holy. When you experience that type of holiness, you cannot think of anything but, wow, He is awesome. To know that you are in the presence of a Holy God. The Holy One of Israel does live. From personal experience there is nothing but love and once you experience that love, nothing compares to it.

How to Build a Mercy Seat

To build the mercy seat in your life is where He can live or dwell in your heart which is to let Him take control. It is at this point where the fine linen ephod that you are wearing with the linen ephod robe has brought you into the very presence of God Almighty.

As a priest you enter in the Majesty's presence bringing the earthly realm to God's Heavenly realm or known as "the third heaven" (see 2 Co. 12:2). When the Sovereign Majesty comes to you it is heaven coming down to Earth in a physical form that you can sometimes see and feel. It heightens your senses to a degree that I cannot express in human terms. To each person it is different.

It is written that "The fear of Yahweh is the beginning of wisdom. The knowledge of the Holy One is understanding" (Pro. 9:10). To have "fear" of Him is more than just respect, honor, and love for Him it is to know that no matter what happens you understand that your time on Earth is in His hands. It is His grace that allows us to present ourselves to God and because of Jesus to boldly go before the throne of grace (see Heb. 4:16). It is also a time when we will be allowed to present our victory crowns to the King of Kings.

As we are robed with the righteous acts that are done in the Lord's name. The righteous acts that are produced according to His will of love is done towards all humanity and opposes the demonic powers that control unregenerated man is what we must battle. Having the fine linen ephod robe on is what is defined as representing Jesus Christ to the lost. Representing who He is in nature, grace, and love. We are not to condemn the sinner, but we are to allow the Holy Spirit to show His light through us so that the lost may have the Spirit's conviction.

As you wear the linen ephod robe, it envelops you and the colors emanate from you. Let the purple royalty of His scarlet blood bring His blue heavenly realm and His Godly golden nature to reflect the colors of your renewed mature nature. Let wisdom come forth now in Jesus's name. This type of wisdom is Kingly wisdom that is reflected in the robe of righteousness.

PUTTING ON THE FINE LINEN EPHOD ROBE

Holy Spirit in the name of Jesus I put on and sink into the fine linen ephod robe. As I embrace this ephod robe, I acknowledge the fact that I can go boldly to the heavenly mercy seat where God inhabits through prayer. I also ask that wherever I go, I can build this mercy seat of grace where Your presence dwells and I can walk in wisdom and Your reverence. Amen.

Chapter 2: The Robe of Righteousness
Part 1

IN ISAIAH 61:10 IT is written that "I will greatly rejoice in Yahweh! My soul shall be joyful in my God, for he has clothed me with the garments of salvation. He has covered me with the robe of righteousness."

Meh-eel is a garment that is worn over the tunic by men of rank and by David's daughter Tamar.[1] The robe of righteousness is a transitional move from priests to kings. This robe is more than righteousness. It encumbers a more detailed aspect of what pertains to reigning with Christ.

It is assumed that you have put on all the previous garments from *The Melchizedek Priesthood Garments* written by author. These set of robes also mark the transition from just being a "kingdom of priests" (see Rev. 1:6 NASB) to truly being "kings" pursuant to Revelation 1:6 NKJV and starting to reign during this age. This robe is about your commencement through how you conduct yourself in the name of Jesus Christ and how you delegate your given authority. This authority is based on how much Father God has given you. As you grow in maturity of your given authority, the more you will receive.

Delegation of the Robe of Righteousness

The delegation of this robe is where you are ruling and reigning during your lifetime and in the next. Practice starts in your house. Whether you have a family or not it starts at home. It is written "...how could someone who doesn't know how to rule one's own house take care of God's assembly?" (1 Tim. 3:5). The way he conducts himself in his house is the same way he will conduct himself in the house or assembly of God. When a person conducts themselves in righteousness it is because they live a holy life.

The authority is only given by Jesus Christ and those that the Holy Spirit has given as leaders, mentors, and friends in your life. In *Spiritual Warfare - Headquarters-The Heavenlies; The Battlefield-Our Minds!* © 1987 by Derek Prince Ministries–International, published by Whitaker House that he defines authority and that our relationship with Jesus's authority with the effectiveness of its definition:

> Jesus said, "'All authority has [already] been given to Me.' You go, therefore...." What does the "therefore" mean? I understand it to mean, "You go and exercise, on My behalf, the authority that I have already won." Our assignment is to administer the victory, demonstrate the triumph, and exercise the authority that Jesus has won on our behalf. Authority is only effective when it is exercised. If we do not exercise the authority that He has given to us, it remains ineffective.[2]

The authority of the Kingly Mantle

The ruling robe of righteousness is put on to those that are mature in Christ. When this garment is put on and/or used in love or agapao (love in action) it used to build up the immature Christian, present the Gospel of the Kingdom to non-Christians, and warfare against the demonic. We are to have no mercy towards the demonic. The demonic and those that are influenced in one way, or another hate us. It our right to only judge the demons and put them under our feet only in the name of Jesus and no other name. When the demonic is put under our feet we then can crush the serpent's head (see Rom. 16:20 WEB; Gen. 3:15 NIV; Luk. 10:19). The amount of kingly authority from where you begin grows and expands by your increasing relationship with the Holy Spirit.

The more that you are submitted to God and continually abide in Him the devil will run away from you (see Jam. 4:7). With this maturing in ruling comes the place of promotion and advancement which brings the ability to be given more authority in love. It is written in Ephesians 4:14-16 the following about growing in love.

> we may no longer be children, tossed back and forth and carried about with every wind of doctrine, by the trickery of men, in craftiness, after the wiles of error;but speaking truth in love, we may grow up in all things into him who is the head, Christ, from whom all the body, being fitted and knit together through that which every joint supplies, according to the working in measure of each individual part, makes the body increase to the building up of itself in love.

As we continue to grow in love towers one another we become more like Jesus Christ who is the King of kings (see Rev. 17:14). If the kingly authority is given too early in a Christian's walk, they become tyrants and beat the sheep, they usually tend to not love and embrace them where they are at.

The "robe of righteousness" is the first of the two kingly robes that God has given us. The other robe is a "robe of justice." This robe cannot be used without having righteousness working in you in the form of "agapao" love. The robe or "meh-eel" of righteousness has a trifold meaning for the Body of Christ.

THE TRIFOLD MEANING OF "MEH-EEL"

The first fold meaning is between the relationship of Tamar and King David. Tamar was the daughter of King David where King David is symbolizing God the Father in relation to the Church as His children where Tamar represents the Church or Children of God that we are mighty, yet we are loved by Him.

If we look at where it was documented about Tamar where "she had on a robe of many colors, for the king's virgin daughters wore such apparel" (2 Sam. 13:18 NKJV). We are told to "put on the armor of light" (Rom. 13:12) which symbolizes putting on Christ (Rom. 13:14) where we are wrapped in a garment of an everlasting light that portrays the rainbow of life. We are seen as pure virgins by the Lord Jesus in His parable of the ten virgins (see Mat. 25:1-13) having oil in their hands prepared for His coming that we will be presented to Christ Jesus as His Bride being "a pure virgin" (2 Cor. 11:2).

Tamar symbolizes that when we, God's children, are wronged and contaminated by the world through deceit, Jesus will avenge us (see Rom. 12:19). Though Absalom was wrong in killing and taking vengeance on behalf of his sister Tamar's contamination, his father King David, represents Christ (see 2 Sam. 13). Jesus loves the Church and will restore to us our position as being seen as virgins. We will overcome the world and no longer be contaminated with the world and are the firstfruits to God and to the Lamb (see Mat. 25; Rev. 14:4).

This robe of many colors also represents all nations, tribes and languages that are redeemed to God through Jesus's blood (see Rev. 5:9). The robe of righteousness is multicolored like the rainbow which is patterned after the life of Jesus. For a more detailed account of the rainbow in relation to the Believer and the Godhead read *Generation "ZION"* by the author.

The second fold meaning of this robe as used in the kingly manner was by king David that when he was praising God that he was clothed with a robe of fine linen like the Levites who bore the ark, the singers, and Chenaniah the music master *with* the singers also had robes of fine linen (see 1 Chr. 15:27). David is wearing a linen ephod which represents the prophet/priestly mantle that is given to Jesus and His brethren. We are to prophesy with words out of our mouth and instruments as seen throughout Scripture (see 1 Sam. 10:5; 1 Chr. 25:1).

The third part of the trifold meaning about the robe of righteousness also is represented between a covenantal exchange between Jonathan and David. For it is written about their relationship that "Jonathan felt very close to David [^{L}the life/soul of Jonathan was knit/bound to the life/soul of David]. He loved David as much as ·he loved himself [^{L}his own life/soul]... He took off his ·coat [robe; ^{C}perhaps a royal robe] and gave it to David, along with his ·armor [tunic], including his sword, bow, and belt [^{C}an expression of loyalty to David and perhaps even giving him the future kingship]" (1 Sam. 18:1, 4 (EXB)).

There is a connection between Jonathan and David which is how our relationship between Elohim and Jesus's body. "For the entire fullness of God's nature(*of the deity)* dwells bodily(or *nature lives in a human body)* in Christ" (Col. 2:9 HCSB). The same verse is written in the Orthodox Jewish Bible (OJB) "because in Moshiach kol melo Elohim (all the plentitude of G-d) finds its bodily maon la Shechinah (dwelling place for the Shechinah)" (Col. 2:9).

For God the Father loved us more than enough through Jesus Christ so Jesus could maintain all His deity in an Earthly body. We as His body represent Jesus to the Earth which is the plentitude and nature of God the Father by releasing His Shechinah glory through the presence of Holy Spirit. When the glory cloud shows up it is difficult to minister because His love is intoxicating (see 1 Kin. 8:10-13).

There are five things that Jonathan gave David. His robe, armor, sword, bow, and belt.

1. The <u>robe</u> that Jonathan is wearing is symbolized in the robes that are being written about. These robes are meant to be examples of what is declared in the Heavenly realms of God.

1. The <u>armor</u> represents the part of that covenantal exchange

where we receive God's armor and put it on according to Ephesians 6:11 for the reason "that you may be able to resist in the evil day, and having prepared everything, to take your stand" (Eph. 6:17 HCSB). That seems like a fair advantage over the enemy that the Kingdom of God has which is God's armor.

1. The <u>sword</u> is a part of the armor and is the only offensive weapon Paul draws upon when discussing the armor of God in Ephesians 6:10, and 17.

1. The <u>bow</u> is not mentioned in the New Testament armor but is still part of the armor that God exchanges with us as being individual parts of the corporate body of Christ Jesus on Earth. The bow is written in more detail in *The Melchizedek Priesthood Garments* written by the author.

1. The <u>belt</u> or girdle is also mentioned in Ephesians 6:10, and 14 where it is given to us as the belt of truth (see Eph. 6:14).

THE BELT/GIRDLE OF TRUTH

The belt that is wrapped around our waist is the Lord Jesus because He said "I am the..truth..." (Joh. 14:6). Since Jesus is the truth of God's Word, then His truth is the object of our hearts because it is eternal and independent of man's interpretation.

The covenantal exchange that we get then from Jesus is access to the Father's love, the Melchizedek priesthood garments, partakers of the God's garments, armor, sword, bow, and belt for accepting Jesus into our hearts and lives. That seems like a good deal. Every part of the covenant is also a part of Jesus Christ that He gives to as being His Christ on Earth and able to be Christ Jesus to the lost and the wounded in the Body of Christ. To emulate love is surmised in the robe of righteousness is in its usage and application in our daily walk with the Lord and others.

The robe of righteousness is based upon truth, righteousness, wisdom, knowledge, and the fear of the Lord which are all aspects of God revealed in Jesus Christ and the Holy Spirit.

The Truth of the Robe of Righteousness

When Jesus declared that He is the truth, he declared that he was equal to Yahweh of truth (see Psa. 31:5). Below are some versus declaring and describing Jesus as the truth that it was primarily in John's gospel. Why? John's gospel was "written, that you may believe that Jesus is the Christ, the Son of God, and that believing you may have life in his name" (Joh. 20:31). John was also the only apostle that is known in canonical history that leaned on the physical heart of Jesus (see Joh. 21:20).

Upon reflection of John's relationship with Jesus is that we should be wanting to feel His heartbeat. His heart should be in line with our spiritual heart. We are to "hate what is evil; cling to what is good" (Rom. 12:9b NIV). See below for a description of the witnessing of Jesus being the truth of God:

In the beginning was the Word, and the Word was with God, and the Word was God...the Word became flesh, and lived among us. We saw his glory, such glory as of the one and only Son of the Father, full of grace and truth...for the law was given through Moses, grace and <u>truth were realized through Jesus Christ</u> (Jh. 1:1, 14, 17 underline mine).

When answering Pilate that Jesus is a King, He answered:

"You say that I am a king. For this reason I have been born, and for this reason I have come into the world, <u>that I should testify to the truth</u>. Everyone who is of the truth listens to my voice" (Joh. 18:37 underline mine).

Jesus was then acknowledged by a crowd saying that "Teacher, we know that You say and teach rightly, and You do not show personal favoritism, but <u>teach the way of God in</u> <u>truth</u>" (Luk. 20:21 NKJV underline mine) showing that when He taught that He taught God's truth unadulterated, pure, and without partiality. Since the age of twelve, Jesus chose to fulfill the Scriptures that declare "I have chosen the way of truth" (Psa. 119:30a).

Like Jesus, I pray that with God's truths in our hearts that we walk in His ways. I choose the way of truth. Do you choose those ways? What happens when you choose the way of truth?

You are taught His ways so that like Jesus we walk in His truth united in our hearts to fear the name Yahweh (see Psa. 86:11). To fear the name of Yahweh is the final aspect of walking in the truth of the mantle of the robe of righteousness.

THE PATH OF TRUTH

It is written that "All the paths of Yahweh are loving kindness and truth to such as keep his covenant and his testimonies" (Psa. 25:10). Because "Yahweh is near to all those who call on him, to all who call on him in truth" (Psa. 145:18). "For Yahweh's word is right. All his work is done in faithfulness" (Psa. 33:4).

Jesus says about the Old Testament that "this is what I told you, while I was still with you, that all things which are written in the law of Moses, the prophets, and the psalms, concerning me must be fulfilled" (Luk. 24:44). As these truths of the Psalms, and the prophets are being presented I know you will see that as these are pointed to our Lord Jesus, that these apply to us in the following ways.

Jesus is coming in the name of Lord or Yahweh who fulfills the burnt offering requirement needed so He can make with us the everlasting covenant by the direction of the Holy Spirit that our work can be directed in truth (see Isa. 61:8). It is written that "by mercy and <u>truth iniquity is atoned for</u>. By the fear of Yahweh men depart from evil." (Pro. 16:6 underline mine). As Jesus made atonement for our iniquities at the cross is the reason why we should depart from evil by the fear of the Lord.

KEEP THE TONGUE TAMED

The evil that we should depart from is bearing a false witness, lies, and slander. "For my mouth speaks truth. Wickedness is an abomination to my lips" (Pro. 8:7). Then it is written that "lying lips are an abomination to Yahweh, but those who do the truth are his delight" (Pro. 12:22). "With it [the tongue] we bless our God and Father, and with it we curse men, who are made in the image of God. Out of the same mouth comes blessing and cursing" (Jam. 3:9-10a).

Though we are of different genders and nationalities or ethnicities we are still children of Adam and Eve and Noah. For Adam was made in the image and likeness of God (see Gen. 1:26). Adam would have been the first king of the world. As sons of God through Jesus Christ we must make sure that our tongue is tamed (see Jam. 3:8) and that we speak the truth of God's Word to anyone with love. It can be tough love, but it must be the truth given in the way God makes it.

As kings in the domain and Kingdom of God it is written that our conduct should be done in mercy and truth for it preserves the king and by love the King upholds his throne (see Pro. 20:28). With the truth of God's word directing us it preserves us. It makes our spirit man stay alive and causes us to not to fall into traps that keep us away from the love of God.

Jesus has not concealed His lovingkindness and His truth from the great assembly (the Body of Christ)...He has let His loving kindness and His truth continually preserve us (see Psa. 40:10, 11b). Can you say that we are allowing His loving kindness and truth to keep us from sinning? For it is written that we are to keep our hearts with all diligence, for out of it comes the wellspring of life (see Pro. 4:23). As we keep our hearts carefully pure, we are to allow God's loving kindness and truth to come out of our mouths which allows us to use it to help bring about God's mercy.

THE PATHS OF MERCY AND TRUTH

"For Yahweh is good. His loving kindness endures forever, his faithfulness to all generations" (Psa. 100:5) and "For his loving kindness is great toward us. Yahweh's faithfulness endures forever. Praise Yah!" (Psa. 117:2). Are you praising God for what He has done and kept us from eternal death? Are you praising Him for making you part of the ministry that rules in different spheres of life?

"Yahweh, you are my God (Elohim). I will exalt you! I will praise your name, for you have done wonderful things, things planned long ago, in complete faithfulness and truth" (Isa. 25:1). Do you know that the counsels of old are the plans before the foundations of the Earth that we would be part of Jesus Christ's "own house, whose house we are if we hold fast the confidence and the rejoicing of the hope firm to the end" (Heb. 3:6 NKJV)? We are also called the saints and members of the household of God (see Eph. 2:19 NKJV) which is why I encourage to always praise His name no matter what the situation is.

It is the truth of the cross and the resurrection of Jesus that the truth of God is given and revealed (see 1 Cor. 15:1-5). If it was not for believing in that resurrection, why would I write this book? We win! It this truth that we must bind around our neck and write on the tablets of our hearts so that His Word, mercy, and truth do not forsake us (see Pro. 3:3 NKJV). Because of our faith in Christ Jesus we are to work through love and mercy to help establish God's Kingdom of love and mercy before the coming judgment of the world.

mercy and truth have met together

It is written that "mercy and truth meet together. Righteousness and peace have kissed each other. Truth springs out of the earth. Righteousness has looked down from heaven" (Psa. 85:10-11). If you notice that with mercy comes truth. They go hand in hand. They walk together. With truth you must have mercy as well as righteousness and peace. The symbolism of kissing is that it is intimate. The Hebrew word in this context for "kiss" is "naw-shak"[3] and has a root word of "naw-sak" meaning to "kindle or burn."[4] This meaning means from what I can understand is that the intimacy level between truth and righteousness is a burning passion for one another.

It is written that we are to "serve the Lord with reverence or fear, and rejoice with trembling. Kiss the Son, lest He be angry, and you perish *in* the way, When His wrath is kindled but a little. Blessed *are* all those who put their trust in Him" (Psa. 2:11-12 NASB). In the 1995 version of the New American Standard Bible, it is written like this "Worship the Lord with reverence, and rejoice with trembling. Do homage to the Son, that He not become angry, and you perish *in* the way, for His wrath may soon or quickly, suddenly, easily be kindled. How blessed are all who take refuge in Him!" (Psa. 2:11-12 NASB 1995).

CELEBRATING THE FEAST OF TABERNACLES

The truth is when we kiss the Son, we are giving Jesus the homage. Homage is to give a formal public special honor or respect in a person's life.[5] By kissing Jesus we are acknowledging that we serve and worship Him with the reverence due to the King of glory (see Psa. 24). The anger that is being spoken of does not pertain to this day and age. This is future time of the Millennial Kingdom and reign of Jesus and the Saints. Below is the reference of the nations of the Earth worshipping King Jesus and celebrating the Feast of Tabernacles in Zechariah 14:16-19 (NKJV):

> And it shall come to pass *that* everyone who is left of all the nations which came against Jerusalem shall go up from year to year to worship the King, the Yahweh of Hosts, and to keep the Feast of Tabernacles. And it shall be *that* whichever of the families of the Earth do not come up to Jerusalem to worship the King, the Yahweh of Hosts, on them there will be no rain. If the family of Egypt will not come up and enter in, they *shall have* no *rain;* they shall receive the plague with

which the Lord strikes the nations who do not come up to keep the Feast of Tabernacles. This shall be the punishment (sin) of Egypt and the punishment of all the nations that do not come up to keep the Feast of Tabernacles.

The Feast of Tabernacles is the celebration of the return of the Messiah to Earth to fulfill the rescuing of Israel from her enemies. Those that choose not to go up will have to face Jesus's wrath. They will not have His blessings (see below what is prescribed and reviewed in Deuteronomy 16). The Feast is also a time of reflection of the promises of a bountiful harvest that come with it.

- At the Feast of Tabernacles...they [you and your son and your daughter, your male servant and your female servant and the Levite, the stranger and the fatherless and the widow, who *are* within your gates (towns) (see Deut. 16:14 NKJV)] shall not appear before the Lord empty-handed. Every man *shall give* as he is able, according to the blessing of the Lord your God (Elohim) which He has given you (Deu. 16:16-17 NKJV).

- Then Moses goes on to reveal what we are to give the Lord Jesus Christ:

You shall observe the Feast of Tabernacles seven days, when you have gathered from <u>your threshing floor and from your winepress</u>. And <u>you shall rejoice in your feast</u>, you and your son and your daughter, your male servant and your female servant and the Levite, the stranger and the fatherless and the widow, who *are* within your gates. <u>Seven days you shall keep a sacred feast to the Lord your God</u> in the place which the Lord chooses, because the Lord your God (Elohim) will bless you in all your produce and in all the work of your hands, so that you surely rejoice (Deut. 16:13-15 NKJV underline mine).

Please note that this feast involves Elohim, the plurality of God or the Father, Son, and Holy Spirit. It is when the consummation and celebration of His inauguration of the Kingdom on Earth is finalized. The yearly blessings of harvest are to be given to Him as it is written "'bring the whole tithe into the storehouse, that there may be food in my house, and test me now in this,' says Yahweh of Armies, 'if I will not open you the windows of heaven, and pour you out a blessing, that there will not be room enough for'" (Mal. 3:10).

THE 30-60-100 FOLD HARVEST

What a promise that as we continue to give to the Lord everything, for He "is able to do exceedingly abundantly above all that we ask or think, according to the power that works in us" (Eph. 3:20). When the parable of the Sower is explained by Jesus "The Sower sows the word.And these are the ones by the wayside where the word is sown... But these are the ones sown on good ground, those who hear the word, accept *it,* and bear fruit: some thirtyfold, some sixty, and some a hundred" (Mar. 4:14-15, 20 NKJV).

Thirtyfold is the bare minimum on what our harvest will receive. This can also mean that at the thirtyfold you are a child of God and a priest of Melchizedek. The sixtyfold is where you work in mature fulness of the Melchizedek priesthood. The one hundredfold is where you are in the kingly realm of ruling and reigning.

DESTINY AND TRIUMPH OF THE HUNDRED-FOLD

It is by your confession of the word that you proclaim where you are at in your faith in the Lord that it will manifest. With the mantle of the robe of righteousness, you have come into the hundredfold of life. It is the destiny of all that you can manifest your relationship with the Holy Spirit in the power of His resurrection to be conformed to His death that as we die daily, we can live a triumphant and victorious life (see Phi. 3:10; 1 Cor. 15:31, 57; 1 Joh. 5:4).

In *Spiritual Warfare - Headquarters-The Heavenlies; The Battlefield-Our Minds!* © 1987 by Derek Prince Ministries–International, published by Whitaker House defines the meaning of triumph:

> The great essential fact is this: **Christ has already defeated Satan and all his evil powers and authorities totally and forever.**
>
> If you remember nothing else, remember that. Christ has already defeated Satan and all his evil powers and authorities totally and forever. He did that through His death on the cross, through His shed blood, and through His triumphant resurrection.[6]
>
> A triumph is not actually the winning of a victory, it is the celebration and demonstration of a victory that has already been won. Jesus, through His death on the cross, demonstrated to the whole universe His victory over the entire satanic kingdom. However, Jesus did not win that victory for Himself, He did not need it. He won it for us. It is God's purpose that that victory should be worked out and demonstrated through us.[7]

AMBASSADORS OF TRUTH

Going back to Psalms 85:10-11 let us continue to study this passage that it is written that "mercy and truth meet together. Righteousness and peace have kissed each other. Truth springs out of the earth. Righteousness has looked down from heaven" (Psa. 85:10-11).

Truth represents the Bride or the earthly, corporeal Body of Christ accepting our relationship with Jesus, who is represented by the righteousness looking down from heaven. This righteousness is heaven coming down to embody Christians. The passion must be that when someone looks upon us that we can fulfill our calling as ambassadors of Jesus Christ (see 2 Cor. 5:20). To be an ambassador is that we are known by the King and are citizens of that country. Our citizenship is in Heaven (Phil. 3:20) or the heavenly realm. We are like Peter and John that "they had been with Jesus" (Act 4:13).

Can we say that we represent the truth in victory and triumph because we hang around with Jesus? As ambassadors we must speak the truth that "Yahweh says: 'I have returned to Zion, and will dwell in the middle of Jerusalem. Jerusalem shall be called "The City of Truth;" and the mountain of Yahweh of Armies, 'The Holy Mountain.'" (Zec. 8:3 underline mine). "But he who does the truth comes to the light, that his works may be revealed, that they have been done in God" (Joh. 3:21). It is out of this truth that our light will shine. The deeds that we have done will shine brightly because they have been in the name of Jesus for true righteousness's sake. No phony versions or misconstrued truth. Pure, unadulterated, no misconceptions of who Jesus is.

We who are the New Jerusalem, the Bride Christ must be a united city speaking truth and have the relationship with the Holy Spirit that we do not speak a word of our volition. That we must make sure we are continually purifying ourselves. Testing our own words. Making sure that it lines up to what the Bible says. The Bible is the last Word on anything. All prophetic words must line up to the times and seasons given through God's timeline to His return. All things must take place for His return for "this gospel of the kingdom will be preached in the whole world as a testimony to all nations, and then the end will come" (Mat. 24:14 NIV).

I will declare that Jesus will return to natural Jerusalem with spiritual New Jerusalem or the City of Truth coming out of the clouds with Him to rule and reign in the Millennial Kingdom.

THE INTIMACY OF Truth

King Solomon spoke about his father, King David to the Lord that David "You have shown to your servant David my father great loving kindness, because he walked before you in truth, in righteousness, and in uprightness of heart with you" (1 Kin. 3:6)

Solomon in remembrance of his father also spoke the following proverb "he *who* speaks truth declares righteousness" (Pro. 12:17a NKJV) for us to dwell with the Lord Jesus Christ we must have the following characteristics that they need to walk uprightly, working righteousness, and speaks the truth in his heart (see Psa. 15:2).

When we meditate in our minds, write the Word of God in our hearts according to Psalm 119:7 which is written that "I will give thanks to you with uprightness of heart, when I learn your righteous judgments." As David walked with integrity of heart so should we praise the Holy Spirit for illuminating and revealing to our hearts what it means to be upright. With this uprightness of heart comes the knowledge and acceptance that God judges righteously. For it is "the Lord Jesus Christ, who will judge the living and the dead at his appearing and his Kingdom" (2 Tim. 4:1). It is also written that "for to this end Christ died, rose, and lived again, that he might be Lord of both the dead and the living" (Rom. 14:9).

When we walk in the truth of the Son of God, we bear witness that we are bearing the fruit of the Spirit (light) for in it comes righteousness and truth for we are commanded to walk as children of light for we are to find out what is acceptable to the Lord. We are to have no fellowship with the unfruitful works of darkness, but rather expose the unfruitful works (see Eph. 5;8-11) for "in the word of truth, in the power of God; by the armor of righteousness on the right hand

and on the left" (2 Cor. 6:7) that we are called to "walk in truth" (3 Joh. 1:4).

The Spirit of God is saying:

> I rejoice greatly when brethren come and testify of the truth *that is* in you, just as you walk in the truth of My love, mercy, and grace. I have no greater joy than to hear that My children walk in truth (see 3 Joh. 1:3-4). As you are walking in the truth of My resurrection so are you walking in My righteousness and able to delegate the truth of My Word to the world. Let go of all things that entangle you of this worldly religious system and engage in Me so that we can be wrapped together, and I can rapture you to the glory realms of My heart. For I yearn to have My heartbeat with your heart. It is with the integrity of your spirit, soul, and body that I can give you the unlimited realms of agape love, grace, mercy, loving kindness, and peace.

THE INTIMACY OF Righteousness

Since before time God has always been righteous. "Righteousness and justice are the foundation of your throne" (Psa. 89:14a). God has always had a throne and because it was built on righteousness means the builder of it had to be righteous. Job described putting righteousness on as clothing (see Job 29:14) since the earliest known days of recorded history. Since we have the righteousness of Christ Jesus working on our behalf, it is for this reason that we need to be aware that we must work on staying holy.

This again is the aspect of reigning and making decisions in the righteousness of Christ Jesus. "For Yahweh is righteous. He loves righteousness. The upright shall see his face" (Psa. 11:7). We, who are the upright, gaze at His face because of our being made righteous. "Yahweh...hears the prayer of the righteous" (Pro. 15:29) and Jesus said, "therefore I tell you, all things whatever you pray and ask for, believe that you have received them, and you shall have them" (Mar. 11:24). When we walk in righteousness God hears us and will answer because you believe they are answered.

In Hebrews 12:11, righteousness is a peaceable fruit that is yielded or produced because we have been trained in God's Word. That Word produces righteousness. We are thus able to execute royal decrees in righteousness because we love You, we know You, we know who You are, and Your very nature for we are upright in heart.

THE PATH OF RIGHTEOUSNESS

I believe this because "He restores my soul. He guides me in the paths of righteousness for his name's sake" (Psa. 23:3). In the name of Jesus, the Holy Spirit leads us down the path of righteousness. "In the way of righteousness is life; in its path there is no death" (Pro. 12:28) for there is no second death for us who believe in Jesus Christ and walk in His way (see Luk. 9:24; Rev. 2:11). "For God's Kingdom is not eating and drinking, but righteousness, peace, and joy in the Holy Spirit. For he who serves Christ in these things is acceptable to God and approved by men" (Rom. 14:17-18).

As children of the light, He "will make your righteousness shine out like light" (Psa. 37:6) and "my tongue shall talk about your righteousness and about your praise all day long" (Psa. 35:28). "For with you is the spring of life. In your light we will see light. Oh continue your loving kindness to those who know you, your righteousness to the upright in heart" (Psa. 36:9-10). As we seek to stay in Abba's light, we see His light reflected on the truth of what is right and wrong. We know the difference between good and evil because His light directs our path. The Holy Spirit convicts us according to His Word which is faithful and true.

According to Psalm 119:50, 89, 105, and 140 proclaims that Your Word revives us, gives us life, settled in Heaven, a lamp to our feet, a light to our path, pure, and as Your servants we love Your Word. It is what brings us this fountain of life and because you continue to show us your lovingkindness by allowing and ordaining us to be in a righteousness royal covenant with You.

As part of the Generation "ZION" army of God's righteousness it is to be like David and proclaim in Psalm 40:9-10:

> I have proclaimed glad news of righteousness in the great assembly. Behold, I will not seal my lips, Yahweh, you know. I have not hidden your righteousness within my heart. I have declared your faithfulness and your salvation. I have not concealed your loving kindness and your truth from the great assembly.

SONS OF FRESH OIL

Though Psalm 45 is speaking of Jesus, we who will rule with Jesus describes part of our relationship with ruling in righteousness. "Your throne, God, is forever and ever. A scepter of equity is the scepter of your kingdom. You have loved righteousness, and hated wickedness. Therefore God, your God, has anointed you with the oil of gladness above your fellows" (Psa. 45:6-7). If we see this scepter, we use it to execute commands of righteous standards which is based on loving righteousness and hating wickedness according to God's standards. As part of God's chosen people through Christ Jesus, He has anointed us with the oil of gladness.

In Zechariah chapter 4 it gives us a description of the Priest-King rulers in the Amplified version where we are called "sons of fresh oil" that have a continuous supply of oil. In verse 14 "then he [the angels speaking to Zechariah] said, 'These are the two sons of fresh oil [Joshua the high priest and Zerubbabel the prince of Judah] who are standing by the Lord of the whole Earth [as His anointed ones].'"

Please notice that as we are discussing the priestly robes and other garments of the Melchizedekian Priesthood that this is a conglomeration of the representations of Joshua the high priest and

Zerubbabel the prince of Judah. This is the part of the mystery of being "a royal priesthood" (see 1 Pet. 2:9).

As "sons of fresh oil" we "proclaim salvation, who says to Zion, 'Our God reigns!'" (Isa. 52:7 NKJV) and "proclaim the excellence of him who called you out of darkness into his marvelous light" (1 Pet. 2:9). "Blessed are those who keep justice. Blessed is one who does what is right at all times" (Psa. 106:3).

GATES OF RIGHTEOUSNESS

When we continue to walk in righteousness it is a gate that we can enter and continue to enter. It is called the "gates of righteousness" and as we enter through them, we will praise our Mighty King Jesus (see Psa. 118:19-20). Like the psalmist wrote "I will not die, but live, and declare Yah's works" (Psa. 118:17). These gates are comprised of the eye, ear, mouth, and heart gates. Can you say that you will have your gates full of righteousness? Will you live forever by declaring the works of God through Jesus and the power of the Holy Spirit during this age?

VICTORY IN RIGHTEOUSNESS

As a Melchizedekian Priest, I am clothed and robed with righteousness and as a saint of God through Jesus, I shout for joy because of the victories in life He has provided and will continue to provide me and my brethren oh Yah! (see Psalm 132:9). The Psalms declare that "Your righteousness is an everlasting righteousness" (Psa. 119:142a) and that "Your testimonies are righteous forever" (Psa. 119:144a).

And the finality of having the righteousness of the robe of righteousness is as King David wrote "as for me, I shall see your face in righteousness. I shall be satisfied, when I awake, with seeing your form" (Psa. 17:15) because "we look for new heavens and a new earth, in which righteousness dwells" (2 Pet. 3:13). As the Apostle Paul wrote, let us take comfort in this:

But when this perishable body will have become imperishable, and this mortal will have put on immortality, then what is written will happen: "Death is swallowed up in victory.

"Death, where is your sting?

Hades, where is your victory?"

The sting of death is sin, and the power of sin is the law.But thanks be to God, who gives us the victory through our Lord Jesus Christ. Therefore, my beloved brothers, be steadfast, immovable, always abounding in the Lord's work, because you know that your labor is not in vain in the Lord (1 Cor. 15:54-58).

I want you to remember that because of His righteousness we have the victory over sin, death, the grave, and every problem we get in to. Let us be able to exercise this royal authority in the name of Jesus with much grace and wisdom.

PUTTING ON THE ROBE OF RIGHTEOUSNESS PART 1

Holy Spirit in the name of Jesus I put on and sink into this aspect of the robe of righteousness. As I embrace this new robe, I acknowledge the fact that I am righteous because of the imputed righteousness of Jesus Christ to my account. I ask You to mold me into the realm of the 100-fold ministry where You, Jesus, can be like a Jonathon to me where I embrace Your robe, armor, sword, bow, and belt. That I choose to walk in present truth as revealed to me and keep choosing to embrace the truth You have for me. Let me go boldly before the throne of grace where I can love Your righteousness and hate the wickedness that You hate. Please continue to make me a Son of Fresh Oil where I walk in the gates of righteousness, and I have victory. Amen.

Chapter 3: The Robe of Righteousness Part 2

THE INTIMACY OF WISDOM

According to David, part of our heritage in the Lord is that "the mouth of the righteous talks of wisdom His tongue speaks justice" (Psa. 37:30). Solomon goes on to declare that "the lips of the righteous feed many" (Pro. 10:21a) and "the mouth of the righteous produces wisdom" (Pro. 10:31a). God our Father gave us wisdom in His Word, which became reality to us through Jesus Christ. we must heed His instructions (see Pro. 13:1) because Jesus Christ is the wisdom of God revealed to humanity (see 1 Cor. 1:24, 30).

The wisdom we are to seek is the wisdom of God that is personified in the person and love of Jesus Christ (see 1 Cor. 1:24, 30; Col. 2:2-3) whose wisdom was "greater than Solomon" (see Mat. 12:42) that we are to use and wear daily.

THE SPIRIT OF WISDOM AND UNDERSTANDING

Wisdom is personified best in the Old Testament mainly between the books of Proverbs, and Ecclesiastes. The author Solomon describes it from a historical aspect, and applicable aspect. But the origin of wisdom is best described by the prophet Isaiah. Though speaking about Jesus, we as His brothers and part of the body can apply to us.

The Spirit of the Lord shall rest upon Him, The Spirit of **wisdom and understanding**, The Spirit of counsel and might, The Spirit of knowledge and of the fear of the Lord (Isa. 11:2 NKJV bold mine).

If you notice first and foremost that the Spirt is the Spirit of the Father. Second, it rested upon Him. Third, with wisdom it accompanies understanding. Though these are 2 of the 7 Spirits of God mentioned in Revelation 1:4 who are before the throne of Jesus Christ. As Jesus said, the Holy Spirit comes in His name (see Joh. 14:26).

Daniel wrote that "Blessed be the name of God forever and ever; for **wisdom** and might are his" (Dan. 2:20 bold is mine). He goes on to describe the actions of wisdom as "He changes the times and the seasons. He removes kings and sets up kings. He gives wisdom to the wise, and knowledge to those who have understanding" (Dan. 2:21).

The Holy Spirit then allows and controls all kings, presidents, authorities on the Earth to promote His plan for the Kingdom (see Rom. 13:1). It is all part of the plan for Jesus to rule with His saints in the seventh or Millennial age. With the infinite ages to come, we know that God the Father will rule and then the unknown truly begins. How exciting!

God said to mankind "Behold, the fear of the Lord, that is wisdom. To depart from evil is understanding.'" (Job 28:27-28). Here Job declares that to fear the Lord is true wisdom. The understanding of wisdom is the application to depart evil. Why? Because God declares wisdom; for He saw it, prepared the usage of it and searched it out. The word in the Hebrew is the name Adonai for the proper name "Yahweh." I want to point out that the context of the word comes from the word "Adon" or master, owner, when referred to man or God's proper name.[8]

GOD GIVES WISDOM

"He gives wisdom to the wise and knowledge to those who have understanding. He reveals deep and secret things; He knows what *is* in the darkness, and light dwells with Him" (Dan. 2:21c-22 NKJV). When you have wisdom God reveals deep and secret things. That is powerful. Why? Because the person that receives God's secrets is where the light lives and resides in him.

With that the person has knowledge of what is dark so when the secrets are revealed they flow like deep rivers of water that refresh, enlighten, and clear up the mind of those that are willing to receive. For "the words of a man's mouth are like deep waters. The fountain of wisdom is like a flowing brook" (Pro. 18:4).

One of the most famous chapters on wisdom is Proverbs 8. Below is the ending to describe part of who Wisdom is:

> "I, wisdom, have made prudence my dwelling. Find out knowledge and discretion. The fear of Yahweh is to hate evil. I hate pride, arrogance, the evil way, and the perverse mouth. Counsel and sound knowledge are mine. I have understanding and power. By me kings reign, and princes decree justice. By me princes rule, nobles, and all the righteous rulers of the earth. I love those who love me. Those who seek me diligently will find me. With me are riches, honor, enduring wealth, and prosperity. My fruit is better than gold, yes, than fine gold, my yield than choice silver. I walk in the way of righteousness, in the middle of the paths of justice, that I may give wealth to those who love me. I fill their treasuries (Pro. 8:12-21).

Let us look at some key signs to this passage. When a person has wisdom, they have prudence or to have "craftiness and guile in a good sense."[9] This word in Hebrew is a feminine noun pronounced "or-maw." This noun is feminine because national Israel is God's bride and the Church, who is spiritual Israel, is Jesus's bride. Prudence is a result of having wisdom.

GOD'S HEAVENLY WISDOM

Wisdom from God is described to be sound for its counsel is from the Holy Spirit. This again is another passage and confirmation that the rulers and kings that rule over communities or countries are set place in by wisdom, no matter what we want to believe.

When you compare verses 17 and 20-21 that the Spirit of Wisdom loves those that love Him and seek Him diligently. With wisdom it paves the road of righteousness in the middle of the multiple paths of justice. Remember justice is not always fair by human standards, but it is in God's way fair. We may not always understand it, but because He is God, and I am man, His ways and thoughts are better in His infinite realm of wisdom (see Isa. 55:9).

LOVING WISDOM

When we love wisdom, God gives us wealth to fill our treasuries. These treasuries are at times physical, but they are also spiritual. Jesus told us to "lay up for yourselves treasures in heaven, where neither moth nor rust consume, and where thieves don't break through and steal" (Mat. 6:20). Why lay them up there? With wisdom it is written that you will be blessed because:

> Yahweh will open to you his good treasure in the sky, to give the rain of your land in its season, and to bless all the work of your hand. You will lend to many nations, and you will not borrow. Yahweh will make you the head, and not the tail. You will be above only, and you will not be beneath, if you listen to the commandments of Yahweh your God which I command you today, to observe and to do (Deu. 28:12-13).

THE THREE SEASONS OF THE HEART

God wants to bless us for our obedience. To rain in our land is to give us increase in the profession that we choose to walk in according to the desires of our hearts according to the season that the harvest is given. The three seasons are flooding, planting, and harvest. You need to flood your heart with the Word of God or whatever is required for your job, then as you flood it you plant the verses in your heart or memorize the procedure for your work. At the proper time of usage, then you receive the harvest of the heart.

PREPARATIONS OF THE HEART

Solomon writes it like this, "the plans of the heart belong to man, but the answer of the tongue is from Yahweh" (Pro. 16:1). "For Yahweh gives wisdom. Out of his mouth comes knowledge and understanding" (Pro. 2:6). How does wisdom come to us? Again, it is to be reading your Word, and asking the Holy Spirit to give you the understanding of the Wisdom, oh you, the New Jerusalem.

> at the entry doors, she cries aloud: "I call to you men! I send my voice to the sons of mankind. You simple, understand prudence! You fools, be of an understanding heart! Hear, for I will speak excellent things. The opening of my lips is for right things. For my mouth speaks truth. Wickedness is an abomination to my lips. All the words of my mouth are in righteousness. There is nothing crooked or perverse in them. They are all plain to him who understands, right to those who find knowledge. Receive my instruction rather than silver, knowledge rather than choice gold. For wisdom is better than rubies. All the things that may be desired can't be compared to it (Pro. 8:3b-11)

When wisdom calls, it is at the gates of the heart and mind. Paul writes that the peace of God, which surpasses all understanding, will guard our hearts and minds through Christ Jesus (see Phil. 4:7) because without the renewing of our mind our hearts are deceitfully wicked (Rom. 12:2; Jer. 17:9). God's "wisdom rests in the heart of one who has understanding, and is even made known in the inward part of fools" (Pro. 14:33).

THE FOOLISH AND WISE HEART

When a person is foolish, wisdom does not dwell there, and the person acts perverse doing things that are not pleasing to God (see Pro.

14:33; Pro. 8:8). When a person does not have wisdom, there is no fear of the Lord.

Wisdom speaks to use about it from His perspective to us:

> Now therefore, my sons, listen to me, for blessed are those who keep my ways. Hear instruction, and be wise. Don't refuse it. Blessed is the man who hears me, watching daily at my gates, waiting at my door posts. For whoever finds me, finds life, and will obtain favor from Yahweh. But he who sins against me wrongs his own soul. All those who hate me love death (Pro. 8:32-36)

WISDOM'S CHILDREN

Wisdom calls us His children because we do not disdain Him. To disdain means to disregard its value. God says to us "My son, if you will receive my words, and store up my commandments within you, so as to turn your ear to wisdom, and apply your heart to understanding" (Pro. 2:1-2). We are blessed by listening to Wisdom and watching for it at the gates of our hearts. The gates of our hearts are connected to God's throne room where we go to it boldly because of the Cross. We must sometimes wait at the posts of the doors for Wisdom's response because it is not time for the answer.

Once the answer is given it produces life and favor from Abba Father. When Wisdom is not listened to it produces hatred, and the love of death. That death may end physically because you went somewhere when you were not commissioned. Yet, depending on God's wisdom, it may produce the losing of our physical life and entering the Heavenly pearly gates because it was our time (see Act. 21:10b-11; Rev. 21:21).

When we have wisdom, it is because we have inclined our ears to it and applied the understanding to our hearts (see Pro. 2:2). It is because "My mouth will speak words of wisdom. My heart will utter understanding" (Psa. 49:3). We must speak with wisdom and act with it.

WISDOM'S SHIELD

The Spirit of Wisdom "lays up sound wisdom for the upright. He is a shield to those who walk in integrity" (Pro. 2:7). Wisdom is to be used with the shield of faith. This shield protects us from the fiery scheming arrows of the enemy for those who walk the straight and narrow path because they are the upright of God (see Eph. 6:11, 16; Mat. 3:3; Mat. 7:14; Lev. 26:13).

PATHS OF RIGHTEOUSNESS

Wisdom with faith is given "so you may walk in the way of good men, and keep the paths of the righteous. For the upright will dwell in the land. The perfect will remain in it." (Pro. 2:20-21). The paths of righteousness means there are many roads in life that we are given to take that are righteous.

Those roads are the decisions that are God led and not using human wisdom. Those paths are straight and narrow. The straight way means that you give up the perverse ways of the world and live towards God's righteousness.

> For wisdom will enter into your heart. Knowledge will be pleasant to your soul. Discretion will watch over you. Understanding will keep you, to deliver you from the way of evil, from the men who speak perverse things, (Pro. 2:10-12)

Are we letting Wisdom rule our hearts? Are we using discretion in how we conduct our lives? I ask this because the results will be a pleasant soul which will preserve and deliver you from the evil way of the perverse, seducing mankind. "Happy is the man who finds wisdom, the man who gets understanding" (Pro. 3:13). Wisdom helps "to deliver you from the immoral woman" (Pro. 2:16 NKJV). In this day of immorality of men and women as being normal is not what God says is normal. Jesus said before His return that it will be like the days of Noah (see Luk. 17:26).

WISDOM'S FAMILY

We are to "tell wisdom, 'You are my sister.' Call understanding your relative, that they may keep you from the strange woman, from the foreigner who flatters with her words" (Pro. 7:4-5). I encourage you men and women to cleave to Wisdom with all your heart. It is written about he who gets wisdom and understanding:

- He who gets wisdom loves his own soul. He who keeps understanding shall find good (Pro. 19:8).

- Wisdom is before the face of one who has understanding (Pro. 17:24a).

- Whoever loves wisdom brings joy to his father (Pro. 29:3a).

Wisdom's family loves Abba and obeys His wisdom which makes Him rejoice because we have insight into what He has prepared for us. The many paths of Yahweh's wisdom are made up of righteousness, justice, equity (a quality of being fair and impartial). God guards them and preserves the way of His saints (see Pro. 2:8-9). Like Paul and his companions "We speak wisdom, however, among those who are full grown, yet a wisdom not of this world nor of the rulers of this world who are coming to nothing" (1 Cor. 2:6).

THE STRENGTH OF WISDOM

I say this because "wisdom is a strength to the wise man more than ten rulers who are in a city" (Ecc. 7:19). The ten horns of the red serpent of Daniel 7, Revelation 12:3, and Revelation 17 are rulers with no established kingdom yet but have influence in Mystery Babylon's wisdom, religion, and currency. We are about to see it revealed. Like Satan, who is full of pride was taken, Babylon is full of pride and hatred towards Christians and God's people alike. "When pride comes, then comes shame, but with humility comes wisdom" (Pro. 11:2).

Wisdom must be used to make sure we do not rush into things that will be detrimental towards our usage of the Holy Spirit and being Christ Jesus's ambassadors. "But the wisdom that is from above is first pure, then peaceful, gentle, reasonable, full of mercy and good fruits, without partiality, and without hypocrisy" (Jam. 3:17). They are those that walk-in the Heavenly wisdom that is pure and loves His life not until death (see Joh. 12:25). They are willing to forsake all for God's will.

WISDOM'S INHERITANCE

"Wisdom is as good as an inheritance" (Ecc. 7:11a). Peter describes our Heavenly inheritance like this:

> Blessed be the God and Father of our Lord Jesus Christ, who according to his great mercy caused us to be born again to a living hope through the resurrection of Jesus Christ from the dead, to an incorruptible and undefiled inheritance that doesn't fade away, reserved in Heaven for you, who by the power of God are guarded through faith for a salvation ready to be revealed in the last time (1 Pet. 1:3-5).

As you see, our inheritance is incorruptible and undefiled because of the living Jesus Christ. We are kept by the power of God through the faith in the belief in Jesus Christ to be revealed at the end of the age when the Kingdom has been preached to all the world. When we are revealed, it is because we are walking about like "a wise man [that] has great power; and a knowledgeable man increases strength; for by wise guidance you wage your war; and victory is in many advisors" (Pro. 24:5-6 brackets mine). We as a collected man will wage our own war against the enemy of our very lives only in the Name of Jesus, the name above all names and this is done with the Holy Spirit's wisdom.

WARFARE WITH WISDOM

We know that we must have God's truth with wisdom in our fight against the Satanic realm with the Armor of Light. Derek Prince goes in *Spiritual Warfare - Headquarters-The Heavenlies; The Battlefield-Our Minds!* © 1987 by Derek Prince Ministries–International, published by Whitaker House regarding truth that is represented in the Armor of Light in Ephesians 6:14 having "put on the girdle of truth we must put away shame, hypocrisy, religious cliches, and saying and doing things we do not mean."[10]

AN EYE COVENANT

We must make sure that when we walk with Wisdom, we have the Light of Jesus flowing through us. For Jesus said, "the lamp of the body is the eye. Therefore when your eye is good, your whole body is also full of light; but when it is evil, your body also is full of darkness" (Luk. 11:34). Our eye gate must remain pure. I ask you to make a covenant with your eye gate to look at humans through God's eyes. See the person of the opposite gender in a non-lustful way. Keep sin out of your heart. Remember, you house the Holy Spirit. You are the temple of God.

THE HOUSE BUILT WITH WISDOM

"Through wisdom a house is built; by understanding it is established; by knowledge the rooms are filled with all rare and beautiful treasure" (Pro. 24:3-4). Jesus discussing about His sayings declares the following, "everyone therefore who hears these words of mine and does them, I will liken him to a wise man who built his house on a rock. The rain came down, the floods came, and the winds blew and beat on that house; and it didn't fall, for it was founded on the rock" (Mat. 7:24-25).

The rains, floods, and winds that blew are trials and temptations that you overcome because of a firm foundation. The foundations are made up "of repentance from dead works, of faith toward God, of the teaching of baptisms, of laying on of hands, of resurrection of the dead, and of eternal judgment" (Heb. 6:1b-2). "Count it all joy, my brothers, when you fall into various temptations" (Jam. 1:2) because "blessed is a person who endures temptation, for when he has been approved, he will receive the crown of life, which the Lord promised to those who love him" (Jam. 1:12).

WISDOM GIVES A CROWN OF LIFE

We receive a crown a life because "the excellency of knowledge is that wisdom preserves the life of him who has it" (Ecc. 7:12b). It is this life that preserves us. I write not just in physical terms but also spiritual. For some are called to give their lives. Jesus asking John to write down His message to the persecuted Church of Smyrna says, "don't be afraid of the things which you are about to suffer. Behold, the devil is about to throw some of you into prison, that you may be tested; and you will have oppression for ten days. Be faithful to death, and I will give you the crown of life" (Rev. 2:10).

I believe that as part of the priestly garments that it is written that the crown of life is a holy crown of pure gold, and written on it is an inscription *like* the engraving of a signet HOLINESS TO THE LORD tied to it a blue cord, to fasten *it* above on the turban (see Exo. 39:30-31 NKJV). We must be Holy as He is Holy (see Lev. 11:44). Again, this shows us that the Divine nature is mixed with our minds and thoughts that is fasted into the third Heavenly realm of God's abode.

FOUNDATION(S)   OF   WISDOM   AND UNDERSTANDING

We also know the foundation of our house is laid down by Jesus Christ. For Paul wrote to the Corinthians about the foundation:

For no one can lay any other foundation than that which has been laid, which is Jesus Christ. But if anyone builds on the foundation with gold, silver, costly stones, wood, hay, or stubble, each man's work will be revealed. For the Day will declare it, because it is revealed in fire; and the fire itself will test what sort of work each man's work is (1 Cor. 3:11-13).

The "Day" in question is the Judgment Seat of Christ. "For we must all be revealed before the judgment seat of Christ that each one may receive the things in the body according to what he has done, whether good or bad" (2 Cor. 5:10). For it is with those foundations and how we conduct ourselves is how we house the Spirit of Wisdom.

For it is written about the comparison of silver, gold, precious stones, a.k.a. rubies versus wisdom below:

- Receive my instruction rather than silver, knowledge rather than choice gold. For wisdom is better than rubies. All the things that may be desired can't be compared to it (Pro. 8:10-11).

- How much better it is to get wisdom than gold! Yes, to get understanding is to be chosen rather than silver (Pro. 16:16)

VESSELS OF HONOR

The comparison here is that gold, silver, and precious stones are nothing compared to wisdom. For with wisdom those foundations must be laid. As Paul wrote to Timothy, let us see what He provides and discusses about foundations of gold, silver, precious stones, wood, and clay:

However God's firm foundation stands, having this seal, "The Lord knows those who are his," and, "Let every one who names the name of the Lord depart from unrighteousness." Now in a large house there are not only vessels of gold and of silver, but also of wood and of clay. Some are for honor, and some for dishonor. If anyone therefore purges himself from these, he will be a vessel for honor, sanctified, and suitable for the master's use, prepared for every good work (2 Tim. 2:19-21).

We can see that there should be no iniquity in the foundation laying. And when the foundations are being laid with gold, silver, wood, and clay they must laid for the vessel of usage of honor or dishonor. It is out of those foundations that our house will be built.

IS STRAW IN YOUR FOUNDATION?

The reason Paul mentions clay to Timothy is a reference to the fact that straw was used to make bricks during the time of Egyptian slavery (see Exo. 5:7). Straw is a non-edible item where Hay is used in edible foods for animals.

The reference to having straw in the foundation means that is filled with worthless non-edible food for human spiritual consumption. The fact that straw is not mentioned can mean two things. Straw by itself is non consumable for human spirituality so it must be thrown into fire that reaps no reward as well as hay. This is a foundation that has no Spiritual value to it. It is worldly or empty wisdom and deceitful to the core.

CLAY VESSELS OF DISHONOR OR HONOR?

The reason why clay is mentioned is a two-fold blessing or curse. Straw mixed with clay as used in Ancient Egypt is a hybrid of human and Godly wisdom which produces vessels of dishonor. When it is pure clay, it is moldable to whatever the Master Builder decides it will be. The width, the length, the height, the breadth of the bricks in the foundation are made of pure clay. When it is heated up and gone through the fire, it is baked, hardened, and usable thus being a vessel of honor. Let us make sure we are sturdy enough with wisdom.

METALLIC VESSELS OF HONOR OR DISHONOR?

The gold and silver are refinable to be used so that they reflect the image of the Master Metal maker. When they are polished, cleaned, and usable they are refined with wisdom thus reflect Jesus and a vessel of honor. When they get corroded with the things of this world, and Jesus is no longer reflected, they become vessels of dishonor. Let us make sure that we desire wisdom above everything else so that we can be the vessels honor with the foundation of gold or silver.

In Melissa Turmino's book *THE ULTIMATE GUIDE TO THE COLORS IN THE BIBLE* she discusses some key facts about Gold:

- Pure gold never tarnishes or reacts.

- Pure gold never needs cleaning.

- Pure gold never ages.

- Our bodies contain about 0.2 milligrams of gold for a 154-pound person, most of it is found in the heart and blood.

- For Gold to be purified it must be heated.[11]

FOUNDATIONS OF TESTED LIKE GOLD

"I... will refine them as silver is refined, and will test them like gold is tested. They will call on my name, and I will hear them. I will say, 'It is my people;' and they will say, 'Yahweh is my God.'" (Zec. 13:9). If you will see that this passage deals with both silver and gold. Let us look at the gold portion. The Lord says that the testing is to make sure that we that we are pure. Looking at the list above shows us that our bodies depend on some portion of the mineral gold.

It is in the heart and blood that gold flows through it. It is by the Divine blood that renews our heart which is given by the Holy Spirit living in us. When we are tested as gold it is that the Holy hottest fire used on the gold is for a certain amount of time. As this times progresses the gold shines brighter and brighter. As we pass more tests, and receive promotions from passing, then we shine brighter and brighter until we are fully consumed by the Light of Jesus Christ.

FOUNDATIONS REFINED AS SILVER

In Zechariah 13:9 God refines us as silver is refined. Yahweh of Armies…"will sit as a refiner and a purifier of silver" (Mal. 3:1, 3) "for he is like a refiner's fire" (Mal. 3:2). It is written that "Yahweh's words are flawless words, as silver refined in a clay furnace, purified seven times" (Psa. 12:6).

The silver that is being tried is that which is the pure spoken word of God. This is letting the living Word, which is more powerful, and sharper than any two-edged sword, which discerns your thoughts and intents of the heart by dividing your soul and spirit and letting His written Word pierce and refine the blemishes of that foundation in your life (see Heb. 4:12).

When we have been purified seven times by the living Word and we reflect His face and are like gold shining brighter and brighter through the testing of the Day of Lord, our foundations have no cracks, God will is that "We are His people" and we will proclaim "Yahweh is my God" (see Zec. 13:9).

We have the wisdom of God (Elohim) shining in and through us because He has been with us during the whole process in the refiner's fire. Where it is His fire of burning off all the chaff and dross of this world; with our old lives that are not in proper alignment with Him.

FOUNDATIONS OF PRECIOUS STONES

The precious stones are used in the foundations that are built into the New Jerusalem of Revelation 21. They have been crushed and refined to the point that they cannot be moved or shaken.

> The foundations of the city's wall were adorned with all kinds of precious stones. The first foundation roas jasper; the second, sapphire; the third, chalcedony; the fourth, emerald; the fifth, sardonyx; the sixth, sardius; the seventh, chrysolite; the eighth, beryl; the ninth, topaz; the tenth,

chrysoprase; the eleventh, jacinth; and the twelfth, amethyst (Rev. 21:19-20).

Every stone has its meaning in place. There are twelve stones that each correspond to an apostle. I am not going to interpret which stone belongs to whom. The meaning is that no matter where you are at in those stones you are loved by God and full of His wisdom. Those precious stones are part of the foundations in your life that are being laid or have been laid down. Foundations can take years to build prior to the finishing of the house or temple that the Holy Spirit is trying to live in.

PUTTING ON THE ROBE OF RIGHTEOUSNESS PART 2

Holy Spirit in the name of Jesus I put on and sink into this aspect of robe of righteousness. As I continue to embrace this robe, I acknowledge that I need Your help to gain wisdom in my life. May my heart become full of wisdom and my mind retain the Word. May I become an honorable vessel. May the foundation of my house where you dwell be refined like silver and pass the tests like gold. As my foundation is also made-up of precious stones may those stones be honorable to You. As You continue to build the house, please remove all straw from my bricks so that I am no longer mixed with worldly wisdom but filled with Heavenly wisdom according to the Scriptures.

Chapter 4: The Robe of Righteousness
Part 3

AT THE END OF MALACHI chapter 3 it is written about those in the book of remembrance. In verses 16-18 it states the following:

> then those who feared Yahweh spoke one with another; and Yahweh listened, and heard, and a book of memory was written before him, for those who feared Yahweh, and who honored his name. They shall be mine," says Yahweh of Armies, "my own possession in the day that I make, and I will spare them, as a man spares his own son who serves him. Then you shall return and discern between the righteous and the wicked, between him who serves God and him who doesn't serve him."

I want to point out that the key to having your name in the book of remembrance is fearing the Lord. For it is written that "the fear of the Lord *is* the beginning of wisdom" (Psa. 111:10a NKJV). Fearing God with respect is the beginning of that wisdom. Then Malachi in verse 16 of the New King James Version goes on to scribe that because we esteem, and/or meditate on His name, who to us Christians is revealed to us as the name of Jesus, He hears and listens to us.

BEING GOD'S PRECIOUS STONES OF WISDOM

The other part to hearing us is that when we become God's precious stones, He will spare us from His coming wrath because we are His children. Which precious stone we become is up to Him for they are used to lay the foundations within us and is our responsibility to use it correctly. With the foundations laid as precious stones we must have it mingled with wisdom.

This heavenly wisdom was to be passed down with the word again, which means we must have lost it and now we have it. The results of the hard-pressed precious stone wisdom is that we can "discern between the righteous and the wicked, between him who serves God and him who doesn't serve him" (Mal. 3:18).

COLLOSIAN PRAYER FOR WISDOM

Like Paul writing to the Church of Colosse, I pray this prayer over you:

> For this cause, we also, since the day we heard this, **don't cease praying and making requests for you, that you may be filled with the knowledge of his will in all spiritual wisdom and understanding**, that you may walk worthily of the Lord, to please him in all respects, bearing fruit in every good work and increasing in the knowledge of God, strengthened with all power, according to the might of his glory, for all endurance and perseverance with joy, giving thanks to the Father, who made us fit to be partakers of the inheritance of the saints in light, who delivered us out of the power of darkness, and translated us into the Kingdom of the Son of his love, in whom we have our redemption, the forgiveness of our sins (Col. 1:9-14 bold mine).

THE INTIMACY WITH THE FEAR OF THE LORD

Isaiah declared about Abba Father, then about Zion and the fear of Yahweh the following:

> Yahweh is exalted, for he dwells on high. He has filled Zion with justice and righteousness. There will be stability in your

times, abundance of salvation, wisdom, and knowledge. The fear of Yahweh is your treasure. (Isa. 33:5-6).

We know that we are the Zion company of Believers in Jesus Christ and that we are filled with God's righteousness and justice. Because we have the wisdom and knowledge of the Holy One in our lives, we are stable and able to acknowledge it in our times of goodness or struggles. The strength of our salvation in Jesus Christ is not limited to time and space, material or immaterial but the riches found in Him. Because of those riches that are abounding in His wisdom is that we should have a healthy fear of the Lord. This fear of Yahweh is His treasure that He shares with us.

Before more is written on this subject of having a healthy fear of the Yahweh that is not limited to the Old Testament but is clearly defined in the Old Testament. It was a prophetic Scripture that defines the Messiah Jesus "**The Spirit of the Lord** shall rest upon Him, the Spirit of wisdom and understanding, the Spirit of counsel and might, the Spirit of knowledge and of the **fear of the Lord** " (Isa. 11:2 NKJV bold mine). Another way of reading this verse is in the World English Bible "**Yahweh's Spirit** will rest on him: the spirit of wisdom and understanding, the spirit of counsel and might, the spirit of knowledge and of the **fear of Yahweh**" (Isa. 11:2 bold mine).

THE SEVEN MANIFOLD SPIRIT OF GOD

If you notice that the 7 manifold Spirit of God is represented as seven Spirits according to Revelation 3:1, 4:5, and 5:6 is before the throne of God. Those Spirits are united as One Spirit that rested upon Jesus at the announcement as God's Son It was at that time that the Holy Spirit descended as a Dove at Jesus's baptism as recorded in Luke 3:22. The manifold Spirit that rested upon Jesus rests upon us and is in us. When we walk with Him, in one way or another the closer we are to Abba, the more the seven Spirits manifest through us. Because Jesus said we would do greater works (see Joh. 14:12).

Remember that the greater works are done by the Holy Spirit. For it is written "how God anointed him [Jesus of Nazareth] with the Holy Spirit and with power, who went about doing good and healing all who were oppressed by the devil, for God was with him" (Act. 10:38 brackets mine). Then when we move in the Holy Spirit's power, not just signs, miracles, and wonders which we should give glory to God for through these happen in the Name of Jesus, but wisdom should move through us. It is by the fact that we exuberate or rejoice gladly and greatly in God's Spirit moving through us by following the six expressions of the Holy Spirit which are: the Spirit of wisdom, the Spirit of understanding, the Spirit of counsel, the Spirit of might, the Spirit of knowledge and of the fear of the Lord or Yahweh .

FEAR PRODUCES LOVE AND OBEDIENCE

Jesus also said "I tell you, my friends, don't be afraid of those who kill the body, and after that have no more that they can do. But I will warn you whom you should fear. Fear him who after he has killed, has power to cast into Gehenna. Yes, I tell you, fear him." (Luke 12:4-5).

It is out of this fear that is more than just having reverence for Him, but it produces love. Jesus loves His Father and loves us that in the garden of Gethsemane that Jesus, "in the days of his flesh, having offered up prayers and petitions with strong crying and tears to him who was able to save him from death, and having been heard for <u>his godly fear</u>,though he was a Son, yet learned obedience by the things which he suffered" (Heb. 5:7-8 underline mine).

The cry was that He did not want to go to the cross. He was scared. He understood the natural fear that man has of death, but He feared God more. It was because of this fear of the Lord that Jesus was able to be successful at the Cross.

Jesus said "Father, if you are willing, remove this cup from me. Nevertheless, not my will, but yours, be done" (Luk. 22:42). He learned to obey Abba Father by the things He suffered. The fear of Yahweh is a lifelong journey. It is this fear or reverence that is not manifested today as it should be.

EXPERIENCING THE FEAR OF THE LORD

The fear of the Lord or Yahweh is more than some cerebral thought to be grasped or just read in the pages of the Old Testament and early Church in the book of Acts. It is something that one must experience in order to truly understand this mystery of the fear of the Lord .

In the YouTube video from *Pure Life Ministries* in the video titled "The Fear of the Lord is the Beginning of Wisdom | 20 Truths that Help the Battle with Porn Addiction" spoken by Steve Gallagher from Mike Yackanelly, he states the following about, in which I am in agreeance what the "The Fear of the Lord" should be in the Christian Church or Christian Community:

> I would like to suggest that the Church become *a place of terror* again; a place where God continually has to tell us, "Fear Not"; A place where our relationship with God is not a simple belief or a doctrine or theology, it is God's burning presence in our lives.

> I am suggesting that the tame God of relevance be replaced by the God whose very presence shatters our egos into dust, burns our sins into ashes, and strips us naked to reveal the real person within.

> The Church needs to become a GLORIOUS DANGEROUS PLACE where nothing is *safe* in God's presence *except us*.

> Nothing-including our plans, our agendas, our priorities, our politics, our money, our security, our comfort, our possessions, our needs.[12]

Steve Gallagher continues to quote Mike Yackanelly from the video titled "The Fear of the Lord is the Beginning of Wisdom | 20 Truths that Help the Battle with Porn Addiction" describes most of the current church:

> We aren't afraid of God, we aren't afraid of Jesus, we aren't afraid of the Holy Spirit. As a result, we have ended up with a *need-centered gospel* that attracts thousands...but transforms no one.[13]

We need a Church that is greater than the first century Church. Paul spoke the following "brothers, children of the stock of Abraham, and those among you who fear God, the word of this salvation is sent out to you" (Act. 13:26). It is also written that "the assemblies throughout all Judea, Galilee, and Samaria had peace, and were built up. They were multiplied, walking in the fear of the Lord and in the comfort of the Holy Spirit" (Act 9:31).

Here it shows that the early Church were actively walking in a relationship that they feared the Lord because of who He is. They saw how people dropped dead, being raised from the dead, and other things that are not fully seen in America mainly because they, the First Century Church, understood the Holiness of the Lord.

THE FEAR OF THE LORD IS WISDOM'S BEGINNING

"The fear of Yahweh is the beginning of wisdom. All those who do his work have a good understanding. His praise endures forever" (Psa. 111:10). Here it shows that if you have wisdom, you have the fear of the Lord or Yahweh. Once you begin to understand that to stand in reverence to a Holy God who loves you, it is awesome and is eternally pure. All you can do is understand that He is Holy. It is out of that Holiness that fear begins. True fear. The fear of the Lord is considered terrible, delightful, and beautiful.

THE FEAR OF THE LORD IS TERRIBLE

I mean terrible because, when the Spirit of the Lord comes in like a mighty rushing wind and the windows of heaven open up, you realize that your flesh is unworthy to be in His presence. No matter where you are at in your life, you fall as a dead man as John did in Revelation 1:17.

From experience when a holy fear comes upon you, there is no doubt that God has entered the room. Nothing is hidden from His sight. When I had this experience in July of 2021, I cried out to the Lord and quoted Isaiah 6:5 (NKJV) "Woe *is* me, for I am undone" without even thinking about it. I asked that my lips be purified because I was so undone. "My flesh trembles for fear of you. I am afraid of your judgments" (Psa. 119:120). It is not judgment of what you have done or not done but it is judgment of your physical flesh against a Holy God. He is heavenly, we are earthly.

Once you experience this aspect of the nature of Abba God, you will never be the same again. The righteous man says "Praise Yah! Blessed is the man who fears Yahweh, who delights greatly in his commandments" (Psa. 112:1). The commandments do not bring you righteousness, they just point them to the Cross where Jesus is our righteousness. "The fear of Yahweh is clean, enduring forever. Yahweh's ordinances are true, and righteous altogether" (Psa. 19:9).

It is when you experience this, that your theology is broken. Another way to look at it is that it is possibly even wrecked. When I came to this point that I understood it is to truly feel clean and that you can endure anything because you know He is there with you. This fear is not to just to terrify you, but also know that He lives in you. As you walk in Him, the fear of the Lord makes itself manifest because people are drawn to His presence. It is the presence that brings humility. Humility that brings about the love of God.

THE FEAR OF THE LORD IS DELIGHTFUL

I encourage you to look at the Brownsville Revival services on YouTube for totally wrecked services that will show God's powerful glory. One portion of the service was uploaded on March 12, 2014, entitled *Brownsville Revival: Glory in the Dark – Part 8*. This service was on June 4, 1998. I ask that as you watch this you have an open heart and intercede for yourself and others. Just concentrate and cry out to the Holy Spirit. Just posture yourself on the floor if you feel you must. The YouTube video is located at the following web IP address: (https://www.youtube.com/watch?v=npdy8kLun9U).

For every child of God's says to themselves that "His delight will be in the fear of Yahweh. He will not judge by the sight of his eyes, neither decide by the hearing of his ears" (Isa. 11:3).That is the way Jesus is. Jesus looks at the heart and intentions of the person. He knows and sees all. But as His children we must delight in the fear of Yahweh or the Lord.

God says, "to man He said, 'Behold, the fear of the Lord, that is wisdom. To depart from evil is understanding" (Job 28:28). God gave us His fear because we behold His majesty. It is also written that "you shall fear Yahweh your God, and he will deliver you out of the hand of all your enemies" (2 Kin. 17:39). You see as you behold the Fear of the Lord, God will deliver you from your enemies. It is one of the reasons that you praise Him. He has fought the battle for you and gives you the victory.

THE FEAR OF THE LORD PRODUCES PRAISE

In *Spiritual Warfare - Headquarters-The Heavenlies; The Battlefield-Our Minds!* © 1987 by Derek Prince Ministries–International, published by Whitaker House:

> Praise calls forth God's supernatural intervention and is also the appropriate response to that intervention...Note the phrase "Awesome in praises." Praise reveals and calls forth God's awesomeness, His fearfulness, especially against the enemies of God's people...Praise is the appropriate response by God's people to His awesomeness, to His fearful acts of war and vengeance on their behalf.[14]

THE FEAR OF THE LORD PROLONGS DAYS

It is written that "the fear of Yahweh prolongs days" (Pro. 10:27a). It just does not extend life but also saves you from things that might hurt you. If you listen to what He has instructed, you then you will have a long life. I will repeat this, if you love God, you will fear Him.

"In the fear of Yahweh is a secure fortress, and he will be a refuge for his children" (Pro. 14:26). Like Israel, their lives were prolonged and saved. They praised Him and they had a place to live. He gave them food, water, and shelter. They were led by Him during their years of rebellion. It was a certain generation that did not rebel, and their lives were spared because they feared Yahweh.

THE FEAR OF THE LORD IS A FOUNTAIN OF LIFE

"The fear of Yahweh is a fountain of life, turning people from the snares of death" (Pro. 14:27). It is this fount of life that gives us eternal life. Out of this fountain flows the blood of Jesus Christ. This life-giving blood that was brought about through His obedience and fear of God.

"If you will fear Yahweh, and serve him, and listen to his voice, and not rebel against the commandment of Yahweh, then both you and also the king who reigns over you are followers of Yahweh your God" (1 Sam. 12:14). The king reigning over you does not just include a literal king or monarch, it would also include a president, a prime minister, etc. But, during those time, no matter what happens, you must not fear death. God will always help you according to His purpose in your life that He has given you.

THE FEAR OF THE LORD JOINS WITH HUMILITY

It might not end up the way you wanted, but it will end up the way He wanted. "The friendship of Yahweh is with those who fear him. He will show them his covenant" (Psa. 25:14). The covenant of the Cross is the first revelation that He gives you. God shares secrets with us, but are we listening and not getting prideful of what He gives us? I ask this because it is with humility that we fear Him. Written below is what two verses say about humility and the fearing of Yahweh:

- The fear of Yahweh teaches wisdom. Before honor is humility (Pro. 15:33).

- The result of humility and the fear of Yahweh is wealth, honor, and life (Pro. 22:4).

THE FEAR OF THE LORD DELIVERS FROM THE SECOND DEATH

It is also written to "behold, Yahweh's eye is on those who fear him, on those who hope in his loving kindness, to deliver their soul from death, to keep them alive in famine" (Psa. 33:18-19). With this fear it will deliver the soul from death and make alive in times of famine is a reference to Joseph and keeping his brothers alive. When things get hard, He will protect us. This covenant saves our souls from the second death. Just know that we should fear Him who can throw us into the lake of fire. But it is out of His love and commitment to us that He does not do this.

"The fear of Yahweh is the beginning of knowledge; but the foolish despise wisdom and instruction" (Pro. 1:7). King Solomon is saying that the fool who is immoral sins against God because he despises the wisdom and instructions that God gives us in His Word to work through our salvation with fear and trembling; for it is God who works in us to will and to do for His good pleasure (see Phil.2:12c-13).

THE FEAR OF THE LORD IS WHERE SECRETS ARE SHARED

This is where the fulfillment of Proverbs 25:2 (NKJV) where it is written that "it *is* the glory of God to conceal a matter, But the glory of kings *is* to search out a matter." It is this reverence and awe that we see who God is in His Word. Experience is just as much needed as the knowledge of it cerebrally. Cerebral or head knowledge is required so when the experience happens, the knowledge of how to apply it is readily available and known.

David then says that it is God who shares His secrets with those that fear Him (see Psa. 25:14 The Living Bible (TLB)). The secrets are written throughout the Scriptures. Those secrets are revealed because as present ambassadorial kings of His imminent glory, we are called to search out into the deep things of God. The deep things are the solid food of the Word (see 1 Cor. 3:2).

THE FEAR OF THE LORD IS HIDDEN TREASURE

Solomon's writes:

> My son, if you will receive my words, and store up my commandments within you, so as to turn your ear to wisdom, and apply your heart to understanding; yes, if you call out for discernment, and lift up your voice for understanding; if you seek her as silver, and search for her as for hidden treasures: then you will understand the fear of Yahweh, and find the knowledge of God. (Pro. 2:1-5)

Like Solomon, Jesus says to incline your ear to Him. To incline means to bow your head in reverence so that you can listen to what He is teaching. It is with discernment of the Holy Spirit that He gives you the Spirit of wisdom and the Spirit of understanding. It is greater than silver and it is the hidden treasures that you must fear God. The hidden treasure is deeper and deeper. It is hidden in the original languages at times that you learn to understand God deeper.

Sometimes studying the pre-Canaanite Hebrew brings a revelation of love, light, and His name to meaning. As, this is not what this is about, I will say, pray and ask for direction on what to listen to and read. Use the discernment from the Holy Spirit to love and fear Him.

FEAR THE NAME OF YAHWEH

The name of the Lord brings His fear. Below are some Scriptures that discuss to fear His name:

- If you will not observe to do all the words of this law that are written in this book, that you may fear this glorious and fearful name, YAHWEH your God (Deu. 28:58).

- So they will fear Yahweh's name from the west, and his glory from the rising of the sun; for he will come as a rushing stream, which Yahweh's breath drives (Isa. 59:19).

- But to you who fear my name shall the sun of righteousness arise with healing in its wings. You will go out, and leap like calves of the stall (Mal. 4:2).

THE SUN OF RIGHTEOUSNESS GIVES HEALING

If you notice that His name is glorious and awesome. Yehovah/ Yahweh Elohim comes about because of the experience and terror He brings. It is His glory that comes in like the rising of the sun and it is His Spirit that lifts up the standard or bar against the enemy that comes in like a flood. He protects you. He heals you because His name is the "The Sun of Righteousness." How powerful that is because He, Jesus, is the true sun that we see in physical form of healing the body in righteous. The sun gives off vitamin D.

We need vitamin D to help the body absorb calcium and phosphate from our diet. These minerals are important for healthy bones, teeth and muscles.

A lack of vitamin D, known as vitamin D deficiency, can cause bones to become soft and weak, which can lead to bone deformities.

In children, for example, a lack of vitamin D can lead to rickets. In adults, it can lead to osteomalacia, which causes bone pain and tenderness.[15]

This shows that as our physical skin needs the sun, just as much as our spiritual man's skin needs the "sun of righteousness" or the "Son of righteousness" that nourishes us with the righteousness of Christ Jesus. He loves us no matter what. It is out of this love that we have mutual love for each other that we can "ascribe to Yahweh the glory due to his name" (Psa. 29:2a) and "worship the Lord in the beauty of holiness" (Psa. 29:2b NKJV). Another way to translate it is "Worship Yahweh in holy array" (Psa. 29:2b WEB).

THE FEAR OF THE LORD PRODUCES TREMBLING

"Oh, worship the Lord in the beauty of holiness! Tremble before Him, all the Earth" (Psa. 96:9 NKJV) or another way to translate it is "Worship Yahweh in holy array. Tremble before him, all the earth" (Psa. 96:9 WEB). If you notice that we are told to worship Yahweh in the beauty of holiness. As previously discussed, the procedure of worshipping Abba, Jesus and the Holy Spirit is first and foremost a heart condition. Then it says to "tremble before Him, all the Earth." That is why I say Jesus is beautiful, delightful, and terrible.

He is beautiful because of His holiness that we are clothed in but is terrible because of His righteousness that He judges the world. This terrifying thought of the Lord Jesus is more horrible to those that have not experienced His love, grace, and mercy than those that have had a radical encounter with Jesus.

As previously mentioned, the terror of the Lord God is based upon a relationship that when heaven invades physical time and space that there is no way that you will question if God is in the house. That terrifying nature of the Lord is glorious because it is what makes your heart tremble.

In Exodus 20:18-21 it is written that the glory of the Lord terrified the people, see below for the recounting of it in Scripture:

> All the people perceived the thunderings, the lightnings, the
> sound of the trumpet, and the mountain smoking. When

the people saw it, they trembled, and stayed at a distance. They said to Moses, "Speak with us yourself, and we will listen; but don't let God speak with us, lest we die." Moses said to the people, "Don't be afraid, for God has come to test you, and that his fear may be before you, that you won't sin." The people stayed at a distance, and Moses came near to the thick darkness where God was.

When God comes down there is a true fear that overcomes you. Do you tremble when God hits the house? Do you tremble and give glory to His name, the name of Jesus? Do you stand afar off, or do you go boldly before the throne of grace? (see Heb. 4:16). Please notice that they saw God and like Moses are we saying, "do not fear; for God has come to be with you, and that His fear may be before you, so that you may not sin." I implore you to please do not willfully sin. He is so worthy of adoration.

We worship Him in the beauty of His holiness because we have been made Holy and can go to Him because of our reverence and love for Him and towards Him. This is a healthy fear that must be produced by love. This final attribute of the Spirit is given last because this is relationally built-in humility.

BE ZEALOUS FOR THE FEAR OF THE LORD

"Do not let your heart be jealous of sinners, but *be zealous* in the fear of Yahweh always" (Pro. 23:17 Legacy Standard Bible (LSB)). To be zealous means to go after it with such tenacity that you do not give up. It is this fear that keeps you in line. It is this love of the fear of Yahweh that delivers you from serving anything other than Jesus. We love Our Heavenly Father.

We do not need to envy those that might be doing better than us because they are sinners and heathens because in the end this is their reward of riches that spoil (see Pro. 17:13; Isa. 3:11). Do not be jealous because this fear is a hidden treasure.

"Who among you fears Yahweh and obeys the voice of his servant? He who walks in darkness and has no light, let him trust in Yahweh's name, and rely on his God" (Isa. 50:10). Jesus is the Lord's servant. We serve Yahweh, Jesus, and the Holy Spirit because God loved us first. It is this love that makes us want to fear or respect and honor Him. David wrote the following:

> What man is he who fears Yahweh? He shall instruct him in the way that he shall choose. His soul will dwell at ease. His offspring will inherit the land. The friendship of Yahweh is with those who fear him. He will show them his covenant (Psa. 25:12-14).

THOSE THAT FEAR THE LORD RECEIVE GUIDANCE

The person that fears God is the one whom the Lord teaches. That is why Jesus said the "the Spirit of truth, has come, he will guide you into all truth, for he will not speak from himself; but whatever he hears, he will speak. He will declare to you things that are coming" (Joh. 16:13) because God chooses whom to teach. That person will live in prosperity, whether it is financial or wisdom and understanding or both shall God bless.

THE FEAR OF THE LORD UNITES OUR HEARTS

That person's descendants will inherit the Earth and the secrets are shared. To share His secrets with us is awesome. "Teach me your way, Yahweh. I will walk in your truth. Make my heart undivided to fear your name" (Psa. 86:11). It is the name that we fear that unites our hearts to Him. Only at the name of Jesus do our hearts unite with God.

Once we have been instructed this is what is also spoken that:

- The fear of Yahweh is to hate evil. I hate pride, arrogance, the evil way, and the perverse mouth (Pro. 8:13).

- The fear of Yahweh leads to life, then contentment; he rests and will not be touched by trouble (Pro. 19:23).

To hate what God hates is to hate evil, pride, arrogance, the evil way of corruption of live and the perverse mouth. Perversion is of Satan. The father of lies is the most wicked spirit this world will ever know. But the fear of the Lord or Yahweh will bring life to those that walk in it and the continual living of it brings satisfaction of life.

INQUIRING IN THE TEMPLE

When we live in the fear of the Lord or Yahweh this will be written on the tablets of your heart (see 2 Cor. 3:3) the following Scripture:

One thing I have asked of Yahweh, that I will seek after:

that I may dwell in Yahweh's house all the days of my life, to see Yahweh's beauty, and to inquire in his temple. For in the day of trouble, he will keep me secretly in his pavilion. In the secret place of his tabernacle, he will hide me. He will lift me up on a rock (Psa. 27:4-5).

When this happens in your life you are seeking God's wisdom through His Word, prayer, and/or a council of Elders in your life. At this place in time, you truly realize that you know the safety of God. You then keep on learning that the Father, Son, and Holy Spirit love's us with impartiality.

Individually, we, the living temple of the Holy Spirit can go to the Heavenly temple and appear before the Father to inquire of problems, questions about "How the beauty of God" relates to our lives in the application of His life in us. It is with this love and inquiry that we get to share in the experience of His daily life in ours.

When we continue to inquire of the Lord we will be shielded from the wickedness of the "accuser of our brothers" (see Rev. 12:10). Because during those days of hardships we will be living in the secret rooms of the Lord. They are filled with treasures that are so vast that they in truly indescribable. Some books have been written by Roberts Liardon, Jesse Duplantis, and Rick Joyner about some of these rooms. I encourage you to seek out those books and read them.

THE REWARD OF GOD'S WORK

The following verses describe God's beauty as being upon us.

- Let your work appear to your servants, your glory to their children. Let the favor of the Lord our God be on us. Establish the work of our hands for us. Yes, establish the work of our hands (Psa. 90:16-17).

- In that day, Yahweh of Armies will become a crown of glory and a diadem of beauty to the residue of his people (Isa. 28:5).

We, the Body of Christ and His servants, God shows us His work in these last days and that His imminent glory comes forth to those that seek Him as His children that He rewards us by showing us His beauty that rests upon us. Are you ready to let it rest upon you? It is this work that is established from generation to generation. The work of our hands is not just physical labor, but it is also spiritual labor. Have you been allowing God to work in your life to build His temple in You so that He has a place to occupy "fully"?

The beauty of the title for Jesus is "captain of our salvation" (see Heb. 2:10 NKJV), the leader of the armies of Heaven, is a crown of glory and His beauty is compared to a diadem for the remnant of the Church that follow His ways with no compromise or progressive thought that alienates us from God and the nation of Israel. The royal diadem is a jeweled crown that we throw at the feet of Jesus because He is worthy to receive all power, glory, and riches (see Rev. 4:10-11).

Now as we have the beauty of the Lord or Yahweh which is received in wisdom and the terrifying love that is eternally bestowed upon us,

His sons and servants, we get to apply this to how we are robed in the righteousness of Jesus.

THE ADMINISTRATION OF THE ROBE OF RIGHTEOUSNESS

The robe of righteousness must be administered with the qualities that pervade in the proper application of the truth of God's Scriptures. It is wisdom greater than Solomon, knowledge and understanding, and co-mingled with the fear of the Lord or Yahweh so that the decisions that are made are with God's justice. It is this justice that the verdicts are rendered or given so that "that each person who belongs to God may be complete, thoroughly equipped for every good work" (2 Tim. 3:17). Yet we are told that "speaking truth in love, we may grow up in all things into him who is the head, Christ, from whom all the body, being fitted and knit together through that which every joint supplies, according to the working in measure of each individual part, makes the body increase to the building up of itself in love" (Eph. 4:15-16). Are you knit or complete in the robe of righteousness? If not, put it on and learn its ways so that when you rule in your life.

PRAYER FOR PERFECTION IN EVERY GOOD WORK

The anonymous writer of the epistle of Hebrews writes this benediction:

> Now may the God of peace, who brought again from the dead the great shepherd of the sheep with the blood of an eternal covenant, our Lord Jesus, make you complete in every good work to do his will, working in you that which is well pleasing in his sight, through Jesus Christ, to whom be the glory forever and ever. Amen (Heb. 13:20-21).

PUTTING ON THE ROBE OF RIGHTEOUSNESS PART 3

Holy Spirit in the name of Jesus I put on and sink into this aspect of the robe of righteousness. As I continue to embrace this robe, I acknowledge that I need the fear of the Lord or Yahweh in my life. I ask that this becomes a reality in my life and the seven manifold Spirits of God become entwined in my life. As I continue to love, respect, and honor Your name Yahweh that You can continue to prosper me with the spiritual blessings that You have given to me before time began. Thank you for rescuing me from the second death. Let Your fear that comes through wisdom continue to guide me into the hidden treasure and secrets of Your Word be a fountain of life in me. May this fountain of life bring forth fruit that no man can take away. Let me be zealous for Your name seeking Your will in my life. I am thankful that I will receive a crown of glory to give you Jesus and favor continue to follow me because I reverence Your name Jesus and thank the Holy Spirit for wrapping me in the robe.

Chapter 5: The Robe of Justice Part 1

IN JOB 29:14 (NKJV) it is written that "I put on righteousness as my clothing; justice was my robe and my turban." As the robe of righteousness was just discussed, now it is time to read about the last robe that is put on, the *Robe of Justice*. The justice of God is more than judgment. It is judgment that is proclaimed as guilty or not guilty not just in a person's life, but also on motives or the actions that an individual renders in their lives.

GOD'S THRONE – THE FOUNDATION OF JUSTICE

Regarding God's eternal, and unmovable throne, Ethan the Ezrahite proclaimed that "righteousness and justice *are* the foundation of Your throne; mercy and truth go before Your face" (Psa. 89:14 NKJV). As with being robed in righteousness, we are also robed in justice as seen as the foundations of God's throne. Again, this robe is communicated to us through a legal royal system. As this is the final robe of the garments that are put on the body, it is also clear to note that when we move through the royal priesthood, we move with certainty, stability, truth, and mercy because we advocate to King Jesus for our fellow human and ourselves.

THE JUDGMENT OF JESUS, NOT THE FATHER

Jesus said, "for the Father judges no one, but he has given all judgment to the Son" (Joh. 5:22). Our Father declares that "For I, Yahweh, love justice. I hate robbery and iniquity. I will give them their reward in truth and I will make an everlasting covenant with them" (Isa. 61:8). As Jesus is the judge of everyone who like His Father loves justice as well as hating robbery and iniquity.

For the true King of the Earth declares "I can of myself do nothing. As I hear, I judge, and my judgment is righteous; because I don't seek my own will, but the will of my Father who sent me" (Joh. 5:30). In other words, as the reflection of God the Father, His judgments are based on what He has heard and seen from God. When Jesus judges it is a righteous judgment. Like Jesus who does the will of Father God so it should be with us. That we seek God's will, not our own.

Jesus speaking to the Pharisees about Himself and the way He judges not according to the flesh (see Joh. 8:15) is that "even if I do judge, my judgment is true, for I am not alone, but I am with the Father who sent me" (Joh. 8:16). Yet, in the following verses Jesus describes His judgments that entail His future prophetic plan of Salvation:

- I have many things to speak and to judge concerning you. However he who sent me is true; and the things which I heard from him, these I say to the world (Joh. 8:26).

- But now I am going to him who sent me, and none of you asks me, 'Where are you going?' But because I have told you these things, sorrow has filled your heart. Nevertheless I tell you the truth: It is to your advantage that I go away, for if I don't go away, the Counselor won't come to you. But if I go, I will send him to you. When he has come, he will convict the world about sin, about righteousness, and about judgment; about sin, because they don't believe in me; about righteousness, because I am going to my Father, and you won't see me any more; about judgment, because the prince of this world has been judged (Joh. 16:5-11).

THE JUDGMENT OF THE HOLY SPIRIT

This is the time that the Holy Spirit judges Mankind for the sin of rejecting of Jesus because of their unbelief in Him. Why? Because they judged as "children of disobedience" (see Eph. 2:2) who walk in the futility of their mind due to ignorance and blindness of their heart (see Eph. 4:17-18). It is the spirits of the antichrist that work in them because they deny God the Father and Jesus the Son (see 1 Joh. 2:22) for we are called to judge angels (see 1 Cor. 6:3). It is the evil spirits that control the evilness of a person. It is written in 2 Cor. 10:3-6:

> For though we walk in the flesh, we don't wage war according to the flesh; for the weapons of our warfare are not of the flesh, but mighty before God to the throwing down of strongholds,throwing down imaginations and every high thing that is exalted against the knowledge of God and bringing every thought into captivity to the obedience of Christ, and being in readiness to avenge all disobedience when your obedience is made full.

OBEDIENCE TO CHRIST FULFILLED

Please note that we are to be ready to punish all disobedience when our obedience to Christ is fulfilled. The obedience is to pull down strongholds, casting down arguments of anything that puts itself higher than the knowledge of God, and to take all thoughts captive. That is true obedience to Christ. This the regenerated Man making sure that we use the double-edged sword of the Spirit as a discerner of the intents of our hearts. This discerner has the ability to cut between the soul and spirit, and of joints and marrow. Meaning that there is no place to hide your thoughts that the living Word cannot penetrate.

It is with this Sword that we use to judge humanity according to the righteousness of Christ. This is where the Spirit of God is used with wisdom and understanding and a lot of mercy and grace. I will repeat, that mercy and grace may save us from a worse punishment than what could have been originally given. If you break the law of the land, you are subject to the laws of that land. No matter what, Jesus will reward you for taking your punishment.

Like Jesus said about our judging, the judging process is not according to the appearance of how things are but judging with righteous judgment (see Joh. 7:24) which is according to the Scriptures.

JESUS THE JUDGE OF EVERYTHING

Before we apply the robe of justice in our lives, we must be able to know Him who said, "'Vengeance belongs to me. I will repay," says the Lord. Again, 'The Lord will judge his people'" (Heb. 10:30). For "He [Jesus] commanded us to preach to the people and to testify that this is he who is appointed by God as the Judge of the living and the dead" (Act. 10:42). Paul reiterated this theme of Jesus being the Judge of the living and the dead in 2 Tim. 4:1 and declared that Jesus was the "Lord of the living and the dead" according to Rom. 14:9. Now we who are living, and called by His name, He will judge us.

When He judges and purges you, it will hurt for a little while, but that time is different individually. "For if we discerned ourselves, we wouldn't be judged. But when we are judged, we are punished by the Lord, that we may not be condemned with the world" (1 Cor. 11:31-32). But I tell you the truth, the freedom obtained cannot be expressed or communicated and conveyed in any human language. It is so vast, this experience, that once it is done, you should never be the same again.

JUDGING GOD'S HOUSE

When we come to a place of maturity with the Lord Jesus that He can entrust us to true judgment say, "Saviors will go up on Mount Zion to judge the mountains of Esau, and the kingdom will be Yahweh's" (Oba. 1:21 bold mine). The mountains of Esau deal with the kingdoms of humanity. While receiving his vision about Joshua the High Priest, the prophet Zechariah reiterates judgment except that it is within God's house. For it is written:

that the Angel of the Lord admonished Joshua, saying 'Thus says the Yahweh of Hosts: "If you will walk in My ways, and if you will keep My command, then you shall also **judge My house**, and likewise have charge of My courts; I will give you places to walk among these who stand here"' (Zec. 3:7 NKJV bold is mine)

When discussing about His house it is in reference to the temple. We are to judge the house of God or the Church's fruit in love. When it is written about His courts it is judiciary or the Church's governmental status that judgement is here. Jesus wants His Courts of Praise back with His beautiful Bride spotless and wrinkle free.

The need is needed so that the congregations are no longer being abused but loved and restored. The judgement will be upon the leaders that have no love or understanding of God's truth and fairness of structure. It is time for the Bride to take her place as celebrating freedom or Jubilee of life and no longer under the control of polluted waters of spiritual earthiness. He wants an unpolluted stream of water that says, "YES JESUS!"

To put the scroll of Obadiah's message was roughly 66 years before Zechariah's visions and messages. As God repeated this and applied it to Joshua the High Priest who is a type and symbol of Jesus Christ and His people, the Church. It is interesting to see how this applies currently and futuristically. In biblestudy.org the following is written about the number 66:

The number 66 derives part of its meaning from the Millennium. Isaiah 66 describes this idyllic time (and beyond) when Jesus Christ will rule over the Earth. Lasting peace will finally come upon Jerusalem and the world's wealth will flow into her (verses 12 - 13). Anyone who does evil upon the Earth will be swiftly dealt with by the Lord and the people shall see his glory (verses 14 - 18).

All the nations on Earth will know God and worship him during the Lord's reign which will number 1,000 years (Isaiah 66:19 - 21). The weekly Saturday Sabbath, instituted by God and kept by the early New Testament church, will continue to be observed (verse 23). These Sabbaths include God's annual Fast Days, which will also be celebrated in their seasons.[16]

Then to walk in God's ways allows us to judge the house of God during this age through wisdom. God allows His entrusted children to judge His house because they walk in the fear of the Lord or Yahweh. With it comes honor because they walk in the humility of Jesus Christ (see Pro. 15:33).

THE THRONE ROOM COURTS

There is another aspect to judging that is in the courts of heaven. These courts are the multilevel throne room where we are allowed to walk among those that are standing in the place of judgment. But this courtroom is made up of the outer court, the inner court, and the holy of holies. It is in the holy of holies that rests the mercy seat of judgment. When we walk among the courts of heaven it is through the power of praise. These verdicts can be proclamations administered in corporate praise and worship about judgment on kings and nations from the demonic world.

JUDGING THROUGH THE SCRIPTURES AND PRAISE

In *Spiritual Warfare - Headquarters-The Heavenlies; The Battlefield-Our Minds!* © 1987 by Derek Prince Ministries–International, published by Whitaker House gives an example on the Believer's administration of judgement:

Praise and God's Word accompany each other when combined are instruments of judgment against kings and nations. The kings and nobles are part of the Spirit world which represents Satan's angelic princes. Using God's Word, which is like a two-edged sword, as God's people, who are called saints are given the privilege to administer the written sentence to those kings and nobles...that authority is based upon God's Word and through the weapon of praise. This administration of God's judgment to the angels, rulers, kings, peoples and nations implies tremendous power and authority.[17]

THE ADMINISTRATION OF JUDGING

This privilege in 1 Corinthians 6:2-3 is written that "don't you know that the saints will judge the world? And if the world is judged by you, are you unworthy to judge the smallest matters? Don't you know that we will judge angels? How much more, things that pertain to this life?" Like a judge in a courtroom that has wisdom, we must judge with that wisdom and fear of Yahweh. The administration that is revealed to us is that which is given through the study and application of the Scriptures that renew your mind daily.

For it is also written in 1 Corinthians 2:13-16 about the wisdom of the Holy Spirit that teaches us the spiritual things and that the Believer that judges all things must be a Spiritual person. That spiritual person is one who is complete and not lacking in wisdom and understanding with spiritual discernment. For it is written:

We also speak these things, not in words which man's wisdom teaches, but which the Holy Spirit teaches, comparing spiritual things with spiritual things. Now the natural man doesn't receive the things of God's Spirit, for they are foolishness to him, and he can't know them, because they are spiritually discerned. But he who is spiritual discerns all things, and he himself is judged by no one."For who has known the mind of the Lord, that he should instruct him?" But we have Christ's mind (1 Cor. 2:13-16).

When speaking about being rightly judged by no one is that the Believer's conduct is blameless. The integrity of the Believer is with honor, and that they are walking in the Spirit which then produces the fruit of the Spirit.

- But the fruit of the Spirit is love, joy, peace, patience, kindness, goodness, faith, gentleness, and self-control. Against such things there is no law (Gal. 5:22-23).

- For you were once darkness, but are now light in the Lord. Walk as children of light, for the fruit of the Spirit is in all goodness and righteousness and truth, proving what is well pleasing to the Lord (Eph. 5:8-10).

YOU MUST INQUIRE TO JUDGE

When you look at verse 10 and the clause of verse 8 that you are walking in the light, which produces the fruit, we are to find out what is acceptable to the Lord. Paul's revelation of this is taken from the Scriptures that "one thing I have asked of Yahweh, that I will seek after: that I may dwell in Yahweh's house all the days of my life, to see Yahweh's beauty, and to inquire in his temple" (Psa. 27:4).

To find out is to inquire in His temple which is to find out what is acceptable to the Lord. In Jesus name we go to the Father, and we are to inquire what are the plans for our daily path. Then those plans should one way or another line up with the Scriptures. Inquiring in the Holy Temple of Father God will produce freedom, give us clarity, or convict us of sin in our life which leads to repentance. If we get convicted, then we should ask immediately for forgiveness and work on not repeating that sin again.

SATAN'S PRIMARY WEAPON AGAINST US

In *Spiritual Warfare - Headquarters-The Heavenlies; The Battlefield-Our Minds!* © 1987 by Derek Prince Ministries–International, published by Whitaker House discusses Satan's primary weapon against the Christian from having victory:

> Satan's primary weapon against us...is guilt...Guilt is the key to our defeat and righteousness is the key to our victory...Because His justice has been satisfied by the death of Christ, He can forgive every sin we have ever committed without compromising His own justice...all our past sinful acts, no matter how many or how serious, have been forgiven when we put our faith in Jesus Christ...provision was made for us to live free from guilt because our faith is reckoned to us for righteousness.[18]

This strategy is used to make us feel that we are inapt to fulfill our calling to judge the things of the demonic and make us believe that we are worthless. But we "may be filled with the knowledge of his will in all spiritual wisdom and understanding, that you may walk worthily of the Lord, to please him in all respects, bearing fruit in every good work and increasing in the knowledge of God" (Col. 1:9b-10). You are worthy because it is reiterated "...walk worthily of God, who calls you into his own Kingdom and glory" (1 The. 2:12).

YOU CAN WALK WORTHILY

Logically then if we are to walk worthy then we must be worthy to be in God's beloved Kingdom. The worthiness then is imputed or given and put on us from our older brother Jesus Christ. The Lord of creation and true giver of life and judge.

For it is written the following about Christ Jesus who is in the Believer's heart and then at the end of the age and the age to becomes Yahweh of Hosts Kingdom:

- For Yahweh is our judge. Yahweh is our lawgiver. Yahweh is our king. He will save us (Isa. 33:22).

- But, Yahweh of Armies, who judges righteously, who tests the heart and the mind,
  I will see your vengeance on them; for to you I have revealed my cause (Jer. 11:20).

Christ Jesus is the one who protects us by being our Judge and King. The saving is partially done for the Christian in the aspect that our human flesh has not been made incorruptible. But as we plead our case to the Judge the vengeance of God comes forth on our enemy. That is part of judging righteously that we can go to the Advocate of our lives when we do not know what to do.

PRAY FOR GRACE AND MERCY ON HUMANITY

He is the only one worthy to provide us with the answer and final defense in our life. It is the mighty name of Jesus that all things are possible because He is God (see Mar. 10:27; Act. 2:32). To make the impossible possible prayer is needed to bring about God's justice. To bring about the Kingly decrees one must be able to work those decrees with grace and mercy. The grace and mercy is for humanity not for the demonic. They are already condemned.

EFFECTIVNESS OF PRAYER

In *Spiritual Warfare - Headquarters-The Heavenlies; The Battlefield-Our Minds!* © 1987 by Derek Prince Ministries–International, published by Whitaker House gives one of the best ways to describe enforcement prayers on God's promises:

But it took prayer to enforce the promises of God's Word. This is what we must understand. The promises of God's word are not a substitute for our prayer, they provoke our prayer, and it takes our prayers to make the promises of

God's Word effective in our spirits. It also takes our prayer to release the intervention of angels on our behalf.[19]

PRAYING FOR ISRAEL AND JERUSALEM

We should be praying for the nation of Israel and the city of Jerusalem. It is written "thus says the Lord of Hosts: 'Behold, I will save My people from the land of the east (rising sun) and from the land of thewest (setting sun); I will bring them *back,* and they shall dwell in the midst of Jerusalem. They shall be My people and I will be their God, in truth and righteousness.'" (Zec. 8:7-8 NKJV). This Scripture is not addressing the Church but the nation of Israel when the veil is lifted from their eyes.

When Paul was revealing the plans of God, he was assuring the Gentiles that the promises of God given to Israel still apply to them. Because "the gifts and the calling of God are irrevocable" (Rom. 11:29). He declared that "all Israel will be saved. Even as it is written, 'There will come out of Zion the Deliverer, and he will turn away ungodliness from Jacob. This is my covenant with them, when I will take away their sins" (Rom. 11:26-27). Then Paul continues that "concerning the Good News, they are enemies for your sake. But concerning the election, they are beloved for the fathers' sake" (Rom. 11:28).

As the Israelites and Jews who are the children of Jacob are only temporarily removed for the opportunity for the Gentiles to be grafted in the true Olive branch of Jesus Christ. This is the nation that Jesus will lead the world into. The customs that were held at the feasts in which He participated in will be our true heritage in the Lord Jesus Christ. AMEN!

Again, the reason why we pray for Jerusalem and the people of Israel currently is based upon the Abrahamic covenant between God and Abraham that "I will bless those who bless you, and I will curse him who treats you with contempt. All the families of the earth will be blessed through you" (Gen. 12:3).

The blessings to the families of the Earth comes from and through the Lord Jesus Christ and His body on Earth. Now this lineage and promise of the blessings to the families of the Earth continues down to Isaac (see Rom. 9:7) and then to Jacob. Because God still says, "I am the God of your father, the God of Abraham, the God of Isaac, and the God of Jacob" (Exo. 3:6).For Jesus repeats Exodus 3:6 in Mat. 22:32 "I am the God of Abraham, and the God of Isaac, and the God of Jacob?' God is not the God of the dead, but of the living."

In the Hebrew the English word of "God" is originally known as the name of "Elohim." In this simple yet profound declaration by Jesus it shows that He Himself is the God of the living. When you apply Jesus in name of "Elohim," He was speaking of Himself. At that moment He was teaching on the resurrection of the dead. Though it was not stated at the time the revelation of His place in the Trinity. It was given in the great commission of baptizing in the name of the Father, Son, and Holy Spirit (see Mat. 28:19). Jesus was inferring that He Himself was also the God of the living and not the dead at that moment.

BLESSINGS OUT OF ZION

As children and descendants of God through Jesus Christ and heirs of the spiritual blessings of Abraham, Isaac, and Jacob. "May Yahweh bless you out of Zion, and may you see the good of Jerusalem all the days of your life" (Psa. 128:5). Then the conditional part of blessing Abba is that you will see your grandchildren (see Psa. 128:6).

The blessing of having a long life, seeing your grandchildren, and not being cursed because of Father Abraham is one of the reasons that we should continually pray for Israel and the city of Jerusalem. "House of Levi, praise Yahweh! You who fear Yahweh, praise Yahweh! Blessed be Yahweh from Zion, who dwells at Jerusalem. Praise Yah!!" (Psa. 135:20-21).

We who have the better covenant and are part of the order of the Melchizedekian priesthood are told to bless Yahweh. He lives and takes up residence in Jerusalem out of His holy mountain Zion. Do you not know that in the natural He will once again through Jesus Christ take up residence in natural Jerusalem as He takes up residence in us, the New Jerusalem? Believe it. Trust in it. It is His Word, not mine.

BUILDING THE TEMPLE OF YOUR HEART

Let Him build the temple of your heart, where He sits and fortifies the New Jerusalem, which lives in your spiritual body. Apply it according to the hymn of A Mighty Fortress surrounding us. This hymn was written by Martin Luther in 1529 and the translation mostly used is by Frederick H. Hedge in 1852. Before you go on reading this, please meditate on this hymn, and ask Abba to give a revelation of the four verses in your heart that apply to your current situation:

VERSE 1

A mighty fortress is our God, a bulwark never failing
Our Helper He, amid the flood of mortal ills prevailing
For still our ancient foe doth seek to work us woe
His craft and pow'r are great, and, armed with cruel hate
On Earth is not his equal

VERSE 2

Did we in our own strength confide, our striving would be losing
Were not the right Man on our side, the Man of God's own choosing
Dost ask who that may be? Christ Jesus, it is He
The Lord of Hosts His name, from age to age the same
And He must win the battle

VERSE 3

And though this world with devils filled should threaten to undo us
We will not fear, for God hath willed His truth to triumph through us
The Prince of Darkness grim, we tremble not for him
His rage we can endure, for lo, his doom is sure
One little word shall fell him

VERSE 4

That word above all Earthly pow'rs, no thanks to them, abideth

The Spirit and the gifts are ours through Him who with us sideth
Let goods and kindred go, this mortal life also
The body they may kill; God's truth abideth still
His kingdom is forever[20]

- Verse 1 declares the strength of God, the position of the devil and his limited power.

- Verse 2 is the declaration of Jesus as the Lord of Hosts and that He must win the battle that is over your life.

- Verse 3 declares that through Jesus Christ we will not fear the devil and that we can endure any challenge that he sends against us. Why? Because we know his time is limited and he is doomed.

- Verse 4 declares the Kingdom of God is eternal. That even if your body dies it is the Spirit that is at our side and God's truth in His word still lives forever no matter what happens.

PUTTING ON THE ROBE OF JUSTICE PART 1

Holy Spirit in the name of Jesus I put on and sink into the robe of justice. Father, I thank you that Your foundation is made up of justice. Jesus as You are my judge, I ask that you judge my heart that it remains pure so that as I execute justice that it is from a pure heart associated with the mercy seat. I release any condemnation and guilt that the enemy has kept me in bondage from the purity of Your heart be removed and that the blood of Jesus be applied for the forgiveness of harboring that condemnation and guilt. Satan, I command you to get your hands off me. You have no power over me and that the chains of guilt have now been broken. These strategic weapons of condemnation and guilt are now over with. I am free in Jesus's name! As a spiritual child of Abraham, Isaac, and Jacob, I accept that until Your return

Jesus, I will be able to have a long life and have the ability of seeing my grandchildren. Bless You oh Yahweh. Praise You Yahweh! Like God's Kingdom that lasts forever, so shall I live eternally in Your presence oh Father God. Blessings to You in Jesus name! Amen.

Chapter 6: The Robe of Justice Part 2

NOW THAT WE KNOW THAT Jesus is the Judge of the living and dead it is written that "Behold, my servant whom I have chosen, my beloved in whom my soul is well pleased. I will put my Spirit on him. He will proclaim justice to the nations" (Mat. 12:18). We are in the time where Jesus is declaring justice to the Gentiles. This is a justice based on the judgment of the coming Day of the Lord. A day that we do not want to see but might. For it is written that we are to "seek Yahweh, all you humble of the land, who have kept his ordinances. Seek righteousness. Seek humility. It may be that you will be hidden in the day of Yahweh's anger" (Zep. 2:3).

Reason of God's Justice

Here we see in a view about what Jesus says, that "blessed are the gentle, for they shall inherit the earth" (Mat. 5:5). The inheritance of the earth is the Millennial Kingdom of Christ and Kingdom of God, which is at hand. It also says that the meek or gentle that holds on to and issues the justice of the Lord will continually seek His righteousness and seek humility. Why? For the protection God will give you during the day of the Lord.

This justice is based on the fulfillment of the entire Bible which is from cover to cover. Not just the New Testament. But it will be when the end of days and Yahweh of Hosts comes down as the Lion of the Tribe of Judah in full battle armor. Leading up to it, it is when the Earth will be as in the days of Noah.

It is when God judges the Earth and the wicked people with multiple judgments or known as Daniel's 70th week or the Great

Tribulation. It is where the Antichrist, the false prophet with Satan as the chief instrument disguise and blind the people of the last age to chase after the occult, denounce Christianity, and pervert Christianity to a way that is not how Jesus intended His body to function.

After that is Armageddon and the coming of King Jesus with His army. Until then, we His body on Earth make war in the Heavenly realms. We rule according to the Spirit of God that lives in us. We rule with justice. Justice based on God character revealed in Jesus Christ, and the living Scriptures declares that the Lord is the habitation of righteousness and justice (see Jer. 50:7 Amplified Classic Edition (AMPC)).

Descriptions of God's Justice

For the declaration about Yahweh being the Supreme God and Lord of lords declares His administration of justice over the satanic/human kingdoms and our relationship to Him in fear and reverence according to Deuteronomy 10: 17-21:

> For Yahweh your God (Elohim) *is* God (Elohim) of gods and Lord of lords, the great God (El), the mighty, and the awesome, who doesn't respect persons or take bribes. He executes justice for the fatherless and widow and loves the foreigner in giving him food and clothing. Therefore love the foreigner, for you were foreigners in the land of Egypt. You shall fear Yahweh your God. You shall serve him. You shall cling to him, and you shall swear by his name. He is your praise, and he is your God, who has done for you these great and awesome things which your eyes have seen.

Then in Deuteronomy 16:19-20a it also confirms the righteousness of God's justice:

> You shall not pervert justice. You shall not show partiality. You shall not take a bribe, for a bribe blinds the eyes of

the wise and perverts the words of the righteous. You shall follow that which is altogether just...

In Job 37:23-24 it is written:

...the Almighty. He is exalted in power. In justice and great righteousness, he will not oppress. Therefore men revere him. He doesn't regard any who are wise of heart.

My Beloved if you review the previous versus that are in Job's time, the Almighty was not able to be found. But in Jesus, we can find the Almighty. It declares His excellent power and that He rules in judgment. That judgment is based in abundance to not oppress us. We who fear the Lord, the Almighty shows no partiality because we seek Him with wisdom in our hearts. I ask this, do you seek Him with wisdom?

Like David Reigned

"David reigned over all Israel; and he executed justice and righteousness for all his people" (2 Sam. 8:15; 1 Chr. 18:14). In Matthew 1:1, Jesus is declared that He is the "son of David" in the genealogy section and by two blind men that He healed that Jesus was also declared the "son of David" (see Mat. 9:27; Mat. 20:30).

Paul writes to the Romans that "concerning his Son, who was born of the offspring of David according to the flesh, who was declared to be the Son of God with power, according to the Spirit of holiness, by the resurrection from the dead, Jesus Christ our Lord through whom we received grace and apostleship for obedience of faith among all the nations for his name's sake; among whom you are also called to belong to Jesus Christ" (Rom. 1:3-6). What this means that like Jesus and David we are to administrate or execute justice and righteousness through the Spirit of holiness. We are to remain holy.

Peter declared to the first Christians, who were Jews, at the Feast of Pentecost the following sermon about Jesus being a prophet, the Christ, His resurrection, and sitting on Father God's throne:

> Brothers, I may tell you freely of the patriarch David, that he both died and was buried, and his tomb is with us to this day.Therefore, being a prophet, and knowing that God had sworn with an oath to him that of the fruit of his body, according to the flesh, he would raise up the Christ to sit on his throne,he foreseeing this spoke about the resurrection of the Christ, that his soul wasn't left in Hades, and his flesh didn't see decay (Act 2:29-31).

It is also written in Isaiah that Jesus, who is the One described, writes about the throne where "in mercy *and* loving-kindness shall a throne be established, and One shall sit upon it in truth *and* faithfulness in the tent of David, judging and seeking justice and being swift to do righteousness" (Isa. 16:5 AMPC).

By birthright Jesus will rule like David with wisdom, strength, honor, and will hasten in righteousness. It is written that "if we endure, we will also reign with him" (2 Tim. 2:12). We are to be like Jesus as we reign on Earth during this life.

This is practice for the millennial reign of Jesus for it is written "but they [the saints] will be priests of God and of Christ, and will reign with Him a thousand years" (Rev. 20:6 brackets mine). This Scripture fulfills what Jesus says about the Overcomer that "<u>he who overcomes, I will give to him to sit down with me on my throne</u>, as I also overcame, and sat down with my Father on his throne" (Rev. 3:21 underline mine). The amount given to us to administrate justice through holiness is based on how developed our relationship is with the Father, Son, and Holy Spirit.

The Throne of God and His Christ

The thrones are a partial extension of God's attributes. We are to administrate justice based upon God's throne. For as one of the "royal psalms" the description of God's throne that "Your throne is established from long ago. You are from everlasting." (Psa. 93:2).

Mike Bickle in *STUDIES IN THE BEAUTY OF GOD – MIKE BICKLE Session 6 Behold a Throne and One Who Sits on It (Rev. 4:2)* describes the two thrones:

> Scripture speaks of two Thrones, the Father's Throne and Jesus' Throne (at His right hand). The two Thrones manifest the one authority of God. The Throne speaks of God's vast Empire or Kingdom.[21]

Mike Bickle, who uses the New King James Version translation of the Bible, also provides four points from *STUDIES IN THE BEAUTY OF GOD – MIKE BICKLE Session 6 Behold a Throne and One Who Sits on It (Rev. 4:2)* about the Thrones:

II. A THRONE AND ONE WHO SAT ON IT

²I was in the Spirit and behold, a Throne set in heaven, and One sat on the Throne. (Rev. 4:2)

A. John sees God's Throne which is far more powerful than the throne of the Roman empire that was crushing Israel and the Church. John sees the Throne and the Person who has total authority over Rome and Satan's kingdom. This revelation brings great confidence to us. A key focus in the Book of Revelation is God's Throne (referred to 40 times).

A. This "set Throne" is set forever. It is not a temporary power like the Roman Empire. God's Throne guarantees us that all of God's plans will come to pass. God's Throne assures us that our destiny cannot be stopped, thus we cannot fail as we relate to Him with faith and obedience. God's will in our life cannot be stopped by Satan, demons or men.

A. The Throne guarantees the certainty of God's plans. The Throne of God is referred to 40 times in the book of Revelation. The Throne pictures God as the ruler over everything; the One who conquers everything. Nothing can resist it and overcome it; it's the highest of all. There are seven Throne scenes in Revelation (4:2-6:17; 7:9-17; 11:15-19; 14:1-5; 15:2-8; 19:1-8; 21:1-22:9).

A. John sees a real Person on the Throne at the governmental center of the universe. A Person with fiery emotions, a vast intellect and who possesses all power, and is 100% observant as He watches over and cares for us. He is a Person who sees, cares, remembers and feels joy or sadness related to our responses to Him. What happens in our life and heart affects His heart. He feels our pain, sees our value, and plans our welfare. We are not alone; we will live together with Him. There is One who desires meaningful partnership with His inferiors.[22]

The Description of God's Throne
The Heavenly Location
Described in the Major Prophets (Isaiah and Ezekiel)

- The Lord *is* in His holy temple; The Lord's throne *is* in heaven (Psa. 11:4a-b).

- Thus says the Lord: Heaven *is* My throne, and Earth *is* My footstool (Isa. 66:1a-b).

- Above the firmament over their heads *was* the likeness of a throne, in appearance like a sapphire stone; on the likeness of the throne *was* a likeness with the appearance of a man high above it (Eze. 1:26).

- And I looked, and there in the firmamentthat was above the head of the cherubim, there appeared something like a sapphire stone, having the appearance of the likeness of a throne (Eze. 10:1).

Described by Jesus

- But I say to you, do not swear at all: neither by heaven, for it is God's throne (Mat. 5:34).

- he who swears by heaven, swears by the throne of God and by Him who sits on it (Mat. 23:22).

Described by the Apostle John

- Behold, a Throne set in heaven, and One sat on the Throne. (Rev. 4:2).

The Heavenly Throne of Jesus Christ, the High Priest

- We have such a High Priest, who is seated at the right hand of the throne of the Majesty in the heavens (Heb. 8:1).

- But to the Son *He says:* "Your throne, O God, *is* forever and ever; A scepter of righteousness *is* the scepter of Your kingdom (Heb. 1:8).

This shows that no matter where we are, in the Heavenly realms is the Father's throne room and Jesus's throne is right beside His.

The Eternality of the Throne

- Your throne, O God, *is* forever and ever; Your throne, O God, *is* forever and ever (Psa. 45:6).

- You, O Lord, remain forever; Your throne from generation to generation (Lam. 5:19).

`The description is that the thrones are eternal and we see them based on human time. The timing of when God created it. His throne existed before time and before all creation. As previously stated, I will repeat, the throne is a partial extension of God's attributes.

PUTTING ON THE ROBE OF JUSTICE PART 2

Holy Spirit in the name of Jesus I put on and sink into the throne aspect of the robe of justice. Father, I thank you that I can reign like King Jesus who has a wisdom greater than Solomon. Thank you for allowing me to understand the revelation of Your Heavenly throne and its eternality. I pray that I have multiple mercy and loving-kindness throne room encounters of Your throne according to the seven Throne scenes according to Revelation (4:2-6:17; 7:9-17; 11:15-19; 14:1-5; 15:2-8; 19:1-8; 21:1-22:9). Amen.

Chapter 7: The Robe of Justice Part 3

THE FOUR ATTRIBUTES of the Throne:
THE ATTRIBUTE OF RIGHTEOUS

"Righteousness and justice are the foundation of his throne"(Psa. 97:2b). As the Judge of all time, King Jesus judges in righteous according to King David it is written that "You sit on the throne judging righteously" (Psa. 9:4b). Remember we have Christ's righteousness imputed to us. The fulfillment is written by Apostle John where he wrote "I saw the heaven opened, and behold, a white horse, and he who sat on it is called Faithful and True. In righteousness he judges and makes war" (Rev. 19:11). You see that Jesus judges by righteousness and will make war according to His righteousness. Jesus still submits to the Father's will.

THE ATTRIBUTE OF JUSTICE

"Righteousness and justice are the foundation of his throne"(Psa. 97:2b). As king Nebuchadnezzar proclaimed about Father God that "now I, Nebuchadnezzar, **praise and extol and honor the King of heaven; for all his works are truth, and his ways justice**; and those who walk in pride he is able to abase" (Dan. 4:37 bold mine).

He is able to humble everyone who set themselves above God by making themselves setup like false gods (see Dan. 3:1-7; 4:1-34). We must pray like the prophet Jeremiah "Yahweh, correct me, but gently; not in your anger, lest you reduce me to nothing" (Jer. 10:24). When we think of justice, we must be able to let the Holy Spirit examine our hearts and allow Him to correct us. Let it be willingly towards Him and let it not be in His anger. This is also a word of warning that though you cannot ever separate yourself from God's love, you can bring judgment to yourself if you rebel and do not repent.

As we wear this robe of justice, this mantle is given from the throne itself. As we ponder on this thought that the robe of justice is also given as a foundational truth of royal justice. We should proclaim with all of Heaven "to him who sits on the throne, and to the Lamb be the blessing, the honor, the glory, and the dominion, forever and ever! Amen!" (Rev. 5:13).

THE ATTRIBUTE OF FIERY LOVE

"His throne was fiery flames, and its wheels burning fire. A fiery stream issued and came out from before him. Thousands of thousands ministered to him. Ten thousand times ten thousand stood before him" (Dan. 7:9e-10b). We also know that "our God is a consuming fire" (Heb. 12:29). Mike Bickle also provides an insight into God's emotions from *STUDIES IN THE BEAUTY OF GOD – MIKE BICKLE Session 6 Behold a Throne and One Who Sits on It (Rev. 4:2)* about the Thrones:

John sees a real Person on the Throne. He is One with fiery emotions and a vast intellect. What happens in our life and heart affects His heart. He cares for us as He sees and remembers our life and struggle. He feels joy or sadness related to our responses to Him. He feels our pain, sees our value, and plans our future blessing, prosperity and happiness. We are not alone. We will live together with Him forever. A real Person desires deep relationship and partnership with us. The Lord carefully takes notice of His friends as well as His enemies. This aspect of His Personhood is hated by the ungodly but is pleasing to those who love Him. He is always watching us. We are always on His mind.[23]

He sees when we endure trials instead of giving up. He sees the positive. He rewards every small act of obedience, especially those hidden from the eyes of others (Mt.6:1-6, 16-18). He remembers and rewards (Heb.6:10). Even small acts, such as giving a cup of cold water, do not go unnoticed by the Lord (Mt. 10:42). Our knowledge of His omniscience persuades us against evil, knowing that it is vain to attempt to hide evil from Him.[24]

THE ATTRIBUTE OF MERCY

Isaiah proclaimed, "then in mercy *and* loving-kindness shall a throne be established, and One shall sit upon it in truth *and* faithfulness in the tent of David, judging and seeking justice and being swift to do righteousness" (Isa. 16:5 AMPC). Jesus declared that "he who rejects Me, and does not receive My words, has that which judges him — the word that I have spoken will judge him in the last day" (Joh. 12:48 NKJV).

If you notice that when He judges it will be in mercy and loving-kindness. For the Christian, the judgment is in mercy and loving-kindness. We have access like those in the age to come that we can "therefore come boldly to the throne of grace, that we may obtain mercy and find grace to help in time of need" (Heb. 4:16).

"You in Your mercy *and* loving-kindness have led forth the people whom You have redeemed; You have guided them in Your strength to Your holy habitation" (Exo. 15:13 AMPC). As the chosen of God through Christ Jesus we are being guided daily in mercy and loving-kindness. For we are redeemed unto God the Father to His holy habitation of Mount Zion. It is in mercy that God will meet us in the holy of holies that is within our hearts (see Exo. 30:6).

The fulness of the trinity is expressed to us that "*He is* the tower of salvation to His king, and shows mercy to His anointed, to David and his descendants forevermore" (2 Sam. 22:51 NKJV). To us, the descendants of King David in the Spirit realm, we are shown mercy by Elohim.

This mercy is unconditional love. It is the mercy that we do not have to face the second death. It is this mercy that we must proclaim Jesus's gift to all humanity. Do you truly believe you have been given mercy? If you do, do not use it as a license to sin. The Lord declares that "He loves you."

HIS MERCY ENDURES FOREVER

In 2 Chronicles 5:12-14 (NKJV) when we praise the Most High and declare that His mercy endures forever in common unity, this is where His glory shows up and no man can withstand it for He is God eternal.

> The Levites *who were* the singers, all those of Asaph and Heman and Jeduthun, with their sons and their brethren, stood at the east end of the altar, clothed in white linen, having cymbals, stringed instruments and harps, and with them one hundred and twenty priests sounding with trumpets — indeed it came to pass, when the trumpeters and singers *were* as one, to make one sound to be heard in praising and thanking the Lord, and when they lifted up their voice with the trumpets and cymbals and instruments of music, and praised the Lord , *saying:*

> "*For He is* good, For His mercy *endures* forever,"

> that the house, the house of the Lord, was filled with a cloud, so that the priests could not continue ministering because of the cloud; for the glory of the Lord filled the house of God.

> "And he [Solomon] said: 'O Lord, God of Israel, there is no god like You in heaven or on the earth, keeping covenant and *showing* mercy *and* lovingkindness to Your servants who walk before You [in

obedience] with all their heart'" (2 Chr. 6:14 AMP). As we walk before God in the covenant of the Cross and resurrection of Jesus Christ with all our hearts, He will extend mercy to us. It is in mercy and grace that He continues to show up with love and great power.

At the dedication of Solomon's Temple, the Lord showed up with love and great power. His shekinah glory came down and filled the temple and the people praised Him and His mercy.

> When Solomon had finished praying, fire came down from heaven and consumed the burnt offering and the sacrifices; and the glory of the Lord filled the temple. And the priests could not enter the house of the Lord , because the glory of the Lord had filled the Lord's house. When all the children of Israel saw how the fire came down, and the glory of the Lord on the temple, they bowed their faces to the ground on the pavement, and worshiped and praised the Lord, *saying:* "For *He is* good, for His mercy *endures* forever" (2 Chr. 7:1-4 NKJV).

I want to ask you, does your physical house get full of God's glory? If it does not, ask Him to fill it. Continue to praise Him because "His mercy *endures* forever."

GOD DESIRES MERCY

God spoke the following in Hosea "for I desire mercy, and not sacrifice; and the knowledge of God more than burnt offerings" (Hos. 6:6). God is saying to us that do not sacrifice things to Him in vanity but desire to obtain mercy for He is merciful and gracious (see Deu. 4:31; 2 Cor. 30:9; Psa. 116:5; Joe. 2:13). "His mercy is for generations and generations on those who fear him" (Luk. 1:50). "For he said to Moses, 'I will have mercy on whom I have mercy, and I will have compassion on whom I have compassion.' So then it is not of him who wills, nor of him who runs, but of God who has mercy" (Rom. 9:15-16).

VESSELS OF MERCY

God has made known to us "and that he might make known the riches of his glory on vessels of mercy, which he prepared beforehand for glory,us, whom he also called, not from the Jews only, but also from the Gentiles?" (Rom. 9:23-24). Are you a vessel of mercy or a vessel of wrath as spoken in Romans 9:23? Like Paul, I choose to be a vessel of mercy. It is out of mercy that we are to walk in the kingly mantle and robe of justice.

MERCIFUL JUDGMENT

James wrote that "judgment is without mercy to him who has shown no mercy. Mercy triumphs over judgment" (Jam. 2:13). We are again to judge by mercy for the judgment in condemnation does not promote love, peace, and joy. For we are to walk in "the wisdom that is from above is first pure, then peaceful, gentle, reasonable, full of mercy and good fruits, without partiality, and without hypocrisy" (Jam. 3:17).

We must remember that "in the past, you were not a people, but now are God's people, who had not obtained mercy, but now have obtained mercy" (1 Pet. 2:10). For we are to maintain a lifestyle in the Spirit for Jude encourages us as the Beloved that we are to build ourselves in the "most holy faith, praying in the Holy Spirit. Keep yourselves in God's love, looking for the mercy of our Lord Jesus Christ to eternal life" (Jud. 1:20-21).

For we are to emulate Jesus because He spoke that we are to "'desire mercy and not sacrifice' for I came not to call the righteous, but sinners to repentance" (Mat. 9:13). For like Jesus the administration of mercy must be first given to the sinners to have repentance. How are you calling sinners to repentance? Fulfill what the Holy Spirit has for you. Repentance is for everyone. I pray that you give mercy to all for all your days and ways.

PUTTING ON THE ROBE OF JUSTICE PART 3

Holy Spirit in the name of Jesus I put on and sink into the mercy aspect of the robe of justice. Abba, I thank you for truly wanting mercy for those that are called in the Olive Tree. I understand that Your throne is made up of four attributes but that You want mercy to be the focus of Your heart. I thank f You that I can and am willing to be a vessel of mercy and honor not dishonor. Lord help me to learn about how to administrate mercy in Jesus name. Amen.

Chapter 8: The Robe of Justice Part 4

THE ADMINISTRATION of Mercy

The administration of mercy is defined by David who wrote in the Psalms about mercy and the relationship between kingship and praising God:

- For the king trusts, relies on, *and* is confident in the Lord, and through the mercy *and* steadfast love of the Most High he will never be moved (Psa. 21:7 AMPC).

- Surely *or* only goodness, mercy, *and* unfailing love shall follow me all the days of my life, and through the length of my days the house of the Lord [and His presence] shall be my dwelling place (Psa. 23:6 AMPC).

- All the paths of the Lord are mercy *and* steadfast love, even truth *and* faithfulness are they for those who keep His covenant and His testimonies (Psa. 25:10 AMPC).

- But I will sing of Your mighty strength *and* power; yes, I will sing aloud of Your mercy *and* loving-kindness in the morning; for You have been to me a defense (a fortress and a high tower) and a refuge in the day of my distress (Psa. 59:16 AMPC).

- I will sing of mercy *and* loving-kindness and justice; to You, O Lord, will I sing (Psa. 101:1).

- But the mercy *and* loving-kindness of the Lord are from everlasting to everlasting upon those who reverently *and* worshipfully fear Him, and His righteousness is to children's children — To such as keep His covenant [hearing, receiving, loving, and obeying it] and to those who [earnestly] remember His commandments to do them [imprinting them on their hearts] (Psa. 103:17-18 AMPC).

REFLECT ON THE PSALMS OF MERCY

As you reflect on the psalms of David about mercy and loving-kindness, we must be able to trust in the Lord . As we follow during our natural life and dwell in God's Temple through prayer His goodness and mercy will follow us. David also declares as we keep His covenant and His testimonies that are written in the Bible and the tablets of our hearts the paths of Lord will be mercy and truth.

The relationship of singing about Yahweh through Jesus and the Holy Spirit our love towards Him is that our song(s) will be about His great power and His mercy. This should be done in the morning or the beginning of our day. When we sing about His mercy and proclaim it, He responds by defending you because you are taking shelter in Abba against those that persecute you and try to hurt you. Because of praising of Yahweh's mercy and justice we get a chance to continually praise Him.

ETERNAL MERCY

David also proclaimed that the mercy of the Lord is eternal to His children that fear Him. For those that fear Him, His righteousness will be seen to their grandchildren to those that keep His covenant of the Cross while remembering to practice His commandments of love. Remember, the 10 commandments are a tutor that point to Jesus Christ, the author and finisher of our faith (see Gal. 3:24; Heb. 12:2).

Solomon wrote in Proverbs about mercy and the ruling king:

- Loving-kindness *and* mercy, truth *and* faithfulness, preserve the king, and his throne is upheld by [the people's] loyalty (Pro. 20:28 AMPC).

- He who earnestly seeks after *and* craves righteousness, mercy, *and* loving-kindness will find life in addition to righteousness (uprightness and right standing with God) and honor (Pro. 21:21 AMPC).

PRESERVED IN MERCY

The wisest man next to Jesus, who is Jesus's physical human ancestor is king Solomon. Under the inspiration of Wisdom, who is the Holy Spirit, writes that the preservation of the king is through mercy, loving-kindness, truth and faithfulness. Righteousness is part of the foundation of God's throne it is no wonder that it is part of a Godly king's preservation of life. Through mercy and truth comes His lovingkindness that the throne of Saintly kings ruling in Christ's likeness is upheld. We who rule must follow righteousness which is declared in the first robe followed by mercy in which they discover that in Christ they have life, righteousness, and honor.

The Saintly Virtuous Woman of Honor

Psalm 149 was written by an unknown author that we are "to execute on them the written judgment. All his saints have this honor. Praise Yah!" (Psa. 149:9). As a saint of the Most High it is written that "the humble in spirit will retain honor" (Pro. 29:23 NKJV). In *The Melchizedek Priesthood Garments*, written by the author, in the chapter entitled *Clothed with "Hode" and "Haw-dawr'" or Splendor and Majesty/Honor*, it is discussed that the Proverbs 31 woman is equivalent to the Bride of Christ. She fights or warfare's in collaboration with her Husband, Jesus Christ. When Solomon writes about the virtuous woman, he discloses a vital role about her that is rendered that "strength and honor *are* her clothing; she shall rejoice in time to come" (Pro. 31:25 NKJV).

This is a forthcoming prophecy that we will rejoice in the future about our clothing. This clothing is based upon the strength that is given to us who "endures to the end will be saved" (Mat. 10:22). Like Paul, I pray that "I take pleasure in weaknesses, in injuries, in necessities, in persecutions, and in distresses, for Christ's sake. For when I am weak, then am I strong" (2 Cor. 12:10). Let us realize that "all who desire to live godly in Christ Jesus will suffer persecution" (2 Tim. 3:12).

The other half of our clothing is based on honor that we receive from our Husband. "If anyone therefore purges himself from these [being vessels of dishonor], he will be a vessel for honor, sanctified, and suitable for the master's use, prepared for every good work" (2 Tim. 2:21 brackets mine). "For this is the will of God, that you abstain from sexual immorality, that each one of you know how to control his own bodyin sanctification and honor,not in the passion of lust, even as the Gentiles who don't know God" (1 The. 4:3-5).

THE WEAKER VESSEL

Peter wrote that "husbands, in the same way, live with your wives according to knowledge, giving honor to the woman, as to the weaker vessel, as also being joint heirs of the grace of life, that your prayers may not be hindered" (1 Pet. 3:7). As our Husband, Jesus Christ is revealed in the passage that He lives in us with understanding. He knows every part of us. The hidden parts of your life that He will reveal and review.

In contrast to us being strong, in aspect of our being weaker vessels, it is based on our current mortality that we are fragile until this perishable body puts on an imperishable body, and mortality puts on immortality (see 1 Cor. 15:53). It is Jesus that honors us, His body because "when one member is honored, all the members rejoice with it" (1 Cor. 12:26).

It written that "the Spirit himself testifies with our spirit that we are children of God; and if children, then heirs: heirs of God and joint heirs with Christ, if indeed we suffer with him, that we may also be glorified with him" (Rom. 8:16-17). Through the strength of enduring sufferings, we will together live the unmerited favor (grace) of life because we are glorified together.

Jesus wants to "present the church to Himself in glorious splendor, without spot or wrinkle or any such thing; but that she would be holy [set apart for God] and blameless" (Eph. 5:27 AMP). The reason for us to be without spot, wrinkle or blemish is that we are to mirror Him because we are washed in the Blood of Jesus and through His Holy Blood it takes away all our sin. It is written that "the blood of Christ, who through the eternal Spirit offered himself without defect to God, cleanse your conscience from dead works to serve the living God" (Heb. 9:14).

FAITHFUL TO CLEANSE US

I ask to reflect and question for yourself if your conscience is cleansed from dead works to serve the living God. Are you allowing the Holy Spirit to cleanse you so that you mirror Jesus and warfare together? If not, it is through repentance and purging of our thought process that we are set free. Release, come out of agreement of anything that entangles you with the things of the ungodly realms of the world. This is anything that leaves you spiritually barren or unfruitful in the knowledge of our Lord Jesus Christ (see 2 Pet. 1:8). Peter writes in his greeting to the Faithful:

> Grace to you and peace be multiplied in the knowledge of God and of Jesus our Lord, seeing that his divine power has granted to us all things that pertain to life and godliness, through the knowledge of him who called us by his own glory and virtue, by which he has granted to us his precious and exceedingly great promises; that through these you may become partakers of the divine nature, having escaped from the corruption that is in the world by lust (2 Pet. 1:2-4).

In the above greeting God is say through Peter that we must have knowledge of God and of our Lord Jesus Christ. That through His divine power we must acknowledge that we have knowledge of Him because of being called out through His glory and virtue. Oh "virtuous woman" we must live in Godliness because we have been given great and precious promises. As partakers of the divine nature of Christ Jesus we have escaped the corruptible ways of the world. Do not be entangled with lust and other forms of sin "but grow in the grace and knowledge of our Lord and Savior Jesus Christ. To him be the glory both now and forever. Amen" (2 Pet. 3:18).

BETROTHED FOR GOOD WORKS

Apostle Peter wrote that as we "grow in grace and knowledge of our Lord and Savior Jesus Christ" (see 2 Pet. 3:18), along with apostle Paul the "apostle to Gentiles" (see Rom. 11:13) wrote to us that "we are his workmanship, created in Christ Jesus for good works, which God prepared before that we would walk in them" (Eph. 2:10). As Jesus is the King, we are betrothed to Jesus Christ. As God the Father is the husband to the physical Israel as it is written: "I will betroth you to me forever. Yes, I will betroth you to me in righteousness, in justice, in loving kindness, and in compassion. I will even betroth you to me in faithfulness; and you shall know Yahweh" (Hos. 2:19-20).

It is written that we are the "Lamb's bride" (see Rev. 21:9). As the bride of Christ, who is also the eternal New Jerusalem according to Revelation 21:1, 10 and we are also spiritual Israel. I will state it like this. As God has a physical people on Earth, so does Jesus on Earth and in Heaven who are the stars that Abraham was foretold about.

When Israel came out of Egypt, God described their population like the "stars of heaven" (see Deu. 10:22 NKJV). As this is the end of the age and there are multitudes of Christians coming out of Egypt, who are citizens of Heaven (see Phil. 3:20) are called the "Israel of God" (see Gal. 6:16 NKJV).

As we are created for Christ Jesus's good works and will be married to Him, we must be joined to Him and be able to execute judgment. We are to make His ways to be our ways, His will our will, His heart our heart. A good example of this is when Jesus was in the Garden of Gethsemane and He was asking the Father to not go to the Cross. Yet He chose to do the Father's will (see Luk. 22:41-43).

JUDGING WITH LOVE AND COMPASSION

As priestly kings that are following what comes from Father God has given to us through the prophet Zechariah which applies to us: "the word of Yahweh came to Zechariah, saying, "Thus says Yahweh of hosts: 'Judge *with* trustworthy justice, and showsteadfast love and compassion *to one another.* You must not oppress *the* widow, *the* orphan, *the* foreigner, and *the* needy. You must not devise evil in your heart *against one another*" (Zec. 7:8-10 Lexham English Bible (LEB)).

In judging with trustworthy justice, we are to show steadfast love and compassion towards each other. The Father goes on to instruct us that we are to "not deprive the foreigner or the fatherless of justice, nor take a widow's clothing in pledge; but you shall remember that you were a slave in Egypt, and Yahweh your God redeemed you there. Therefore I command you to do this thing" (Deu. 24:17-18).

We are to "let justice roll on like rivers, and righteousness like a mighty stream" (Amo. 5:24). How do we do this? By letting the Holy Spirit use us and flow like streams of living water through us (see Joh. 7:38).

EXECUTE JUSTICE AND RIGHTEOUSNESS

"The Lord Yahweh says: 'Let it suffice you, princes of Israel: remove violence and plunder, and execute justice and righteousness; dispossessing my people,' says the Lord Yahweh" (Eze. 45:9). We as princes of God must execute God's justice and righteousness without killing our brother or sister in Christ. We must not belittle one another but love one another. Embrace their faults and love them as Jesus loves them. Love them with mercy and grace.

When you see your brother or sister fall from grace we must not be like the enemies and accusers who slander each other. From prophet Micah's point of view about Israel's confession and comfort it is written:

> Don't rejoice against me, my enemy. When I fall, I will arise. When I sit in darkness, Yahweh will be a light to me. I will bear the indignation of Yahweh, because I have sinned against him, until he pleads my case, and executes judgment for me. He will bring me out to the light. I will see his righteousness (Mic. 7:8-9).

Will you plead your brother or sister's case with them and help them ask for justice? Will you go before the throne of grace and ask for mercy? It is out of mercy that grace is given. Will you make sure the light is restored to your fellow Christian? I implore you to be like this.

> But you have come to Mount Zion, and to the city of the living God, the heavenly Jerusalem, and to innumerable multitudes of angels, to the festal gathering and assembly of the firstborn who are enrolled in heaven, to God the Judge of all, to the spirits of just men made perfect, to Jesus, the mediator of a new covenant, and to the blood of sprinkling that speaks better than that of Abel (Heb. 12:22-24).

Do you realize that as part of the general assembly we are to lead people to the Mediator of the new covenant at any time they ask? Lead them. Let them receive mercy like you do. That is the justice of this time towards those that believe in Him. There is mercy. For it is written we are to take those that have been like the following. "If a man is caught in some fault, you who are spiritual must restore such a one in a spirit of gentleness; looking to yourself so that you also aren't tempted" (Gal.

6:1). I implore you to help restore those that need restoration in love, gentleness, and mercy.

JESUS'S FUTURE EARTHLY JUDGMENT

We preach the gospel because Jesus will come to make war against Babylon the Harlot and the Anti-Christ. Solomon wrote from a personal point of view, in which, we as Christians should believe like him that "I said in my heart, 'God will judge the righteous and the wicked; for there is a time there for every purpose and for every work'" (Ecc. 3:17). "For Yahweh will execute judgment by fire and by his sword on all flesh" (Isa. 66:16).

As King Jesus wears the robes of righteousness and justice, He will execute true justice and judgment. It is written that when Jesus comes back that "the nations were angry, and your wrath came, as did the time for the dead to be judged, and to give your bondservants the prophets, their reward, as well as to the saints, and those who fear your name, to the small and the great, and to destroy those who destroy the earth" (Rev. 11:18).

If you notice again, He is coming to reward the prophets, the saints, and those that fear His name. There is another connection that we are to fear the name of Jesus. This fear for us that He loves us and yet His presence is terrifying. The terror that you live to come closer to Him in Spirit and truth. The type of closeness that is only gained through relationship and love.

The gentiles hate Jesus because they are against anything that opposes their way of thinking and proclaiming their Satanic kingdom. That is a false kingdom where Christ will take vengeance upon it. The gentiles walk "in lewdness, lusts, drunken binges, orgies, carousings, and abominable idolatries" (1 Pet. 4:3).

Jesus disclosed about what He will do at the end of the age as the Judge:

But when the Son of Man comes in his glory, and all the holy angels with him, then he will sit on the throne of his glory. Before him all the nations will be gathered, and he will separate them one from another, as a shepherd separates the sheep from the goats. He will set the sheep on his right hand, but the goats on the left. Then the King will tell those on his right hand, 'Come, blessed of my Father, inherit the Kingdom prepared for you from the foundation of the world; for I was hungry and you gave me food to eat. I was thirsty and you gave me drink. I was a stranger and you took me in. I was naked and you clothed me. I was sick and you visited me. I was in prison and you came to me (Mat. 25:31-36).

GOAT AND SHEEP NATIONS

Jesus is coming to establish His physical throne and divide the kingdoms of this Earth between sheep and goat nations (see Mat. 25:32). The sheep nations are those that serve Jesus, and the goat nations are those that are cursed and do not serve Jesus. I ask you will you pray for your nation to become a sheep nation?

The goat nations have leaders/kings that are abominations because they commit wickedness. A true throne is established by righteousness (see Pro. 16:12).

The sheep nations have leaders/kings that seek righteousness, practices God's will, and will acknowledge the Theocratic rule of Jesus through the Holy Spirit during this age. The throne of Jesus is established in righteousness before the foundations of the ages.

FUTURE THEOCRATIC RULERSHIP OF JESUS

This shows what Solomon prophesied about Jesus that "a king who sits on the throne of judgment scatters away all evil with his eyes" (Pro. 20:8). "Yahweh's eyes are everywhere, keeping watch on the evil and the good" (Pro. 15:3).

It is this reason that we must be able to know that Jesus knows all that we do. Because "Yahweh has made his holy arm bare in the eyes of all the nations" (Isa. 52:10a). Remember this, that our Jesus in Hebrew is Yeshua and declares that He is also Elohim or God of all the nations. "All the ends of the earth have seen the salvation of our God" (Isa. 52:10b). The reading of this verse translated from Hebrew is that the earth shall see "Yeshua Elohim."

King Jesus will take away those that are wicked that are before the king, and his throne will be established in righteousness (see Pro. 25:5). It is these "wicked kings and nations" or "goat nations" that will be taken away and the righteous throne with the establishment of Jesus's throne.

Solomon declares that "mercy and truth preserve the king, and by lovingkindness he upholds his throne" (Pro. 20:28 NKJV). As Jesus reigns currently in us and in the future, it is in mercy and the truth of His word and by His lovingkindness at the Cross that Spiritual and physical thrones are established.

JUDGMENT OF THE POOR WITH TRUTH

When our King, Jesus, "who fairly judges the poor, his throne shall be established forever" (Pro. 29:14). This shows that Jesus's throne is eternal because "didn't God choose those who are poor in this world to be rich in faith, and heirs of the Kingdom which he promised to those who love him?" (Jam. 2:5). Below it is written about the Judgment of Jesus:

> But Yahweh reigns forever. He has prepared his throne for judgment. He will judge the world in righteousness. He will administer judgment to the peoples in uprightness (Psa. 9:7-8).

the inauguration of the Millennial Kingdom

With the inauguration of the Millennial Kingdom and the establishment of Jesus's throne and His Christ's throne, with the Body of Christ will be physically announced by the seventh angel:

> Then the seventh angel sounded: And there were loud voices in heaven, saying, "The kingdoms of this world have become *the kingdoms* of our Lord and of His Christ, and He shall reign forever and ever!" And the twenty-four elders who sat before God on their thrones fell on their faces and worshiped God,saying:
>
> "We give You thanks, O Lord God Almighty,
>
> The One who is and who was and who is to come,
>
> Because You have taken Your great power and reigned.
>
> The nations were angry, and Your wrath has come,
>
> And the time of the dead, that they should be judged,
>
> And that You should reward Your servants the prophets and the saints,
>
> And those who fear Your name, small and great,
>
> And should destroy those who destroy the earth."
>
> Then the temple of God was opened in heaven, and the ark of His covenant was seen in His temple. And there were lightnings, noises, thunderings, an earthquake, and great hail (Rev. 11:15-19)

JESUS LOVES YOU, NEED OF REPETENCE?

Jesus will judge and there will be an open heaven. Do you not know that what we know is still in part? Do you not know that He who judges the dead and the living loves you? If you need to rededicate your life to Jesus because you have misjudged someone, please ask Him to forgive you. I do not want you to be left out of the first resurrection where we will reign with Jesus for 1,000 years (see Rev. 20:6). My brother or sister please note that He wants you. He loves you. I cannot reiterate that the power of true love wants you to reign with Him.

Final Judgment

Please note that at the end of time that those who choose not to follow Jesus and allow Him to use them for good works will be judged for final judgment after the first resurrection. Apostle John made a description before the endless ages at the Great White Throne:

> Then I saw a great white throne and Him who sat on it, from whose face the earth and the heaven fled away. And there was found no place for them. And I saw the dead, small and great, standing before God, and books were opened. And another book was opened, which is *the Book* of Life. And the dead were judged according to their works, by the things which were written in the books.The sea gave up the dead who were in it, and Death and Hades delivered up the dead who were in them. And they were judged, each one according to his works (Rev. 20:11-13).

I want you to notice that the judgment was based upon each person's works. Those were works that were not good works that were created for Jesus. It is on this account that they were damned because their names were not written in the Book of Life. Jesus says to us "let your light so shine before men, that they may see your good works and glorify your Father in heaven" (Mat. 5:16). It is "for this reason the gospel was preached also to those who are dead, that they might be judged according to men in the flesh, but live according to God in the spirit" (1 Pet. 4:6 NKJV).

Can you magnify Jesus and give an account of the reason for the gospel in your life? Tell them of the coming disaster for this current time of COVID and what is yet to come. I also want you to remember the following Scriptures about King Jesus does for us:

> Sing praises to Yahweh, who dwells in Zion, and declare among the people what he has done. For he who avenges blood remembers them. He doesn't forget the cry of the afflicted (Psa. 9:11-12).

Beloved know that as Jesus sends His angels to help you during your time of need. There is a future time of physical vengeance that will happen on your behalf. He avenges you but during this time please reflect on the beginning of this chorus proclaims that we are to sing praises. Use the garment of praise and declare what Jesus has done for you and what will happen to the enemy.

Tell the wicked of where you were. Then you can tell them where you are going. Remember when Satan had you bound to sin and anything that was not God that Jesus set you free. Praise Him! Dance, sing, play musical instruments! You have been delivered. Whatever form of praising you do, do it to please the King and the King only.

WORSHIP WITH A MIND OF MERCY

As a praise and worshipper before and for the Living Elohim, I pray that you look at this song that was written by Lindell Cooley called *"Kyrie" (Lord Have Mercy)*. This song was played live at the Brownsville Revival in Pensacola, Florida where I know it will bless you if you listen to this version on YouTube (*https://www.youtube.com/watch?v=V7d2GFbp-pc*). The theme is about mercy and revival. This is what America, and the rest of the nations need! Mercy oh Lord we cry out to You!

As you continue to praise and worship the King of Glory keep yourselves humble and know that this is not a competition on who can praise and/or worship better or who can love more. It is about knowing that your heart is right before King Jesus and that you are His.

PRAYER OF OUR ETERNAL KINGDOM POSITION

In our humility comes the realization that "I am persuaded that neither death, nor life, nor angels, nor principalities, nor things present, nor things to come, nor powers, nor height, nor depth, nor any other created thing will be able to separate us from God's love which is in Christ Jesus our Lord" (Rom. 8:38-39). Because "the kingdom and the dominion, and the greatness of the kingdoms under the whole sky, will be given to the people of the saints of the Most High. His kingdom is an everlasting kingdom, and all dominions will serve and obey him" (Dan. 7:27 underline mine).

PUTTING ON THE ROBE OF JUSTICE PART 4

Holy Spirit in the name of Jesus I put on and sink into the administration portion of the mercy aspect of the robe of justice. I thank you for showing me mercy and that I can administrate mercy to all that need mercy. May the mercy that has been given to me be given to those that need it. I hope that through the testimony of the blood of Jesus and my testimony that I can lead those that you put in my path to Jesus Christ. Make me a faithful witness. Thank you for allowing me to rule now and in the millennial Kingdom where I will be sitting and administrating where You need me. Amen.

PART II – THE HUMILITY OF THE PRIEST

Chapter 9: Clothed With Humility (Part 1)

PETER WROTE TO "**clothe yourselves with humility**, to subject yourselves to one another; for "God resists the proud, but gives grace to the humble" (1 Pet. 5:5 bold mine). This clothing is a garment that must be put-on over-all the garments, robes, and the armor of God/Light.

Rick Joyner in *The Final Quest* describes the reason for having the "cloak of humility" cover the armor of God that you wear:

> I could not make out what I was seeing because the glory shining from my armor made it difficult to see into the darkness. I asked Wisdom if there was something that I could cover my armor with so I could see it. He then gave me a very plain mantel to put on.

> "What is this?" I inquired, a little insulted by its drabness.

> "*Humility,*" said Wisdom. "*You will not be able to see very well without it.*"

> Reluctantly I put it on, and immediately I saw many things that I could not see before. I looked toward the valley and the movement I had seen. To my astonishment, there was an entire division of the enemy horde that was waiting to ambush anyone who ventured from the mountain.

"What army is that?" I asked, "and how did they escape the battle intact?"

"*That is Pride*," explained Wisdom. "*It is the hardest enemy to see after you have been in the glory. Those who refuse to put this cloak on will suffer much at the hands of that most devious enemy.*"[25]

There are three things I want to point out about this cloak/mantle of humility.

- First, it is plain to look at and not what you expect it to look like.

- Second, it is needed to see clearly in the Spirit realm.

- Third, it causes you to have discernment.

What does the cloak look like?

The vision I received on what this cloak looks like is equivalent to what John the Baptist's garment of camel skin is. John himself was clothed in camel's hair (see Mat. 3:4; Mar. 1:6). Why a camel? According to Leviticus 11:4 and Deuteronomy 14:7 the camel is considered unclean to eat. It is also considered a beast of burden (see Isa. 30:6).

The reason for camel's hair was that it was prophetic of three things.

First for God takes what is unclean and makes it clean. For "what God has cleansed, you must not call unclean" (Act. 10:15).

Second, Jesus says from His throne that "behold, I am making all things new" (Rev. 21:5). We are no longer beasts or unclean gentiles but part of the heavenly company that we are surrounded with (see Heb. 12:1). Though He is speaking of a new heaven and new earth, we are prophetically living there.

I write this because where Jesus is, so are we. If we are seated in heavenly places in Christ Jesus (see Eph. 2:6) then according to the prophetic word of God, we are partially living in the new heaven and new earth. We can then proclaim that though we live in this present age that we are citizens and a people of the new heaven and earth (see Rev. 21:1).

Third, Jesus said "take my yoke upon you and learn from me, for I am gentle and humble in heart; and you will find rest for your souls. For my yoke is easy, and my burden is light" (Mat. 11:29-30). This yoke is not difficult like a harsh task masker. Our Lord Jesus through the Holy Spirit teaches us all things through His Word and gives our hearts hope for full future redemption of peace. Though we wage war, we wage war in the supernatural not the natural.

OVERCOMING TEMPTATIONS

If we have the yoke of Christ on us, this message reflects that we are His bondservants like Jude (see Jud. 1:1 NASB). We are interconnected to Jesus because we are part of His body because He is the head that we are to grow into (see 1 Cor. 12:27; Eph. 4:15).

Once we are connected to Him, we then take on His burden. Traditionally it is meant that what He puts on us is easy to take and that He will not give us more than what we can bear. That is corrupted teaching. The passage is taken from 1 Corinthians 10:13 that says, "no temptation has taken you except what is common to man. God is faithful, who will not allow you to be tempted above what you are able, but will with the temptation also make the way of escape, that you may be able to endure it." The context of this verse is about having temptations in life and not going through life easy breezy.

This is also stating that He will give you a way of escape but until that point comes, you must bear it or endure it. "But now Yahweh who created you...and he who formed you...says: 'Don't be afraid, for I have redeemed you. I have called you by your name. You are mine. When you pass through the waters, I will be with you, and through the rivers, they will not overflow you. When you walk through the fire, you will not be burned, and flame will not scorch you. For I am Yahweh your God, the Holy One of Israel, your Savior'" (Isa. 43:1-3b).

This passage states that we are the Savior's people and that He is with us when we are going through the fires and storms of life that include temptations. The Holy Spirit will guide us through them. But the warning is that we do not become prideful about judging our brethren that are going through temptations unless they become overwhelmed by it and become engrossed in that sin (see 1 Cor. 10:12; Gal. 6:1).

the law of the Spirit of life

In Galatians 6:2 we are prescribed a remedy for helping the burdens of our brother and sisters that we are to "bear one another's burdens, and so fulfill the law of Christ." The law of Christ is written in Romans 8:2 that "the law of the Spirit of life in Christ Jesus made me free from the law of sin and of death." Through the Holy Spirit we are given life that makes us free from a spiritual law of sin and a spiritual and natural law of death.

It is written that "as sin reigned in death, even so grace might reign through righteousness to eternal life through Jesus Christ our Lord" (Rom. 5:21). Now we know that "God is love" (1 Joh. 4:8) and that in Ephesians 2:4-7, written below, states that our position in love leads us beyond the law of sin and death.

> But God, being rich in mercy, for his great love with which he loved us, even when we were dead through our trespasses, made us alive together with Christ—by grace you have been saved— and raised us up with him, and made us to sit with him in the heavenly places in Christ Jesus,that in the ages to come he might show the exceeding riches of his grace in kindness toward us in Christ Jesus.

RESTORATION OF BRETHREN

We know that we are living in heavenly realms and raised up to life spiritually and the natural to come that when we help restore our brethren that we lead them back to the light of life. As we bring them back to the light remember and be encouraged that we are to "fight the good fight of faith. Take hold of the eternal life to which you were called" (1 Tim. 6:12)" We must fight with and alongside our brethren since we are brothers and sisters in arms. Just remember that our weapons are mighty (see 2 Cor. 10:4).

When we fight, we fight in humility according to Colossians 3:12-15 that,

> as God's chosen ones, holy and beloved, a heart of compassion, kindness, lowliness, humility, and perseverance; bearing with one another, and forgiving each other, if any man has a complaint against any; even as Christ forgave you, so you also do. Above all these things, walk in love, which is the bond of perfection. And let the peace of God rule in your hearts, to which also you were called in one body, and be thankful.

HUMILITY BRINGS UNITY

The cloak of humility brings unity. This shows that when we are united, we can put on the tender mercies, kindness, humility, meekness, longsuffering of Jesus Christ. Jesus said to the Pharisees, "as the Father knows me, and I know the Father. I lay down my life for the sheep. I have other sheep, which are not of this fold. I must bring them also, and they will hear my voice. They will become one flock with one shepherd" (Joh. 10:15-16).

We are then united in unconditional love (agape) which is what bonds us together, making us perfect in His sight. This unconditional love that Jesus tells us to have in Greek according to John 15:12 is that "this is my commandment, that you love one another, even as I have loved you." The Greek word for love in this verse is "agapao", as previously written about in *Generation "ZION"* by the author, is an unconditional love towards each that is continually moving. To apply this verse in our lives, let us read it from this point of view that as Jesus's commandment towards us that we have an active unconditional love with each other as He has an active unconditional love with us.

With the agapao (active unconditional love) we must continue to put on humility. "For Yahweh takes pleasure in his people. He crowns the humble with salvation" (Psa. 149:4). Jesus takes pleasure in His Church that He will glorify/beautify those that are humble with salvation.

BEAUTIFYING the humble with salvation

David Guzik in the web article *PSALM 149 – THE HIGH PRAISES OF GOD AND A TWO-EDGED SWORD* expounds about beautifying the humble with salvation:

> i. "Not only does God take a personal interest in each step of the obedient soul, but He makes it beautiful, and leads it from victory to victory." (Meyer)

> ii. "The qualification for receiving Jehovah's help is meekness, and the effect of that help on the lowly soul is to deck it with strange loveliness." (Maclaren)

> iii. "God taketh pleasure in all his children as Jacob loved all his sons; but the meek are his Josephs, and upon these he puts the coat of many colours, beautifying them with peace, contentment, joy, holiness, and influence." (Spurgeon)[26]

To summarize the quotes given above from three authors: Frederick Brotherton Meyer, Alexander Maclaren, and Charles Haddon Spurgeon write when God beautifies you, He leads from the point of victory. As a Christian, by submitting ourselves to God in all humility in His sight, with the notion of loving Him with adoration towards Him for what He has done and will do for you will cause Abba to lift you up and exalt you (see Jam. 4:10). As God takes pleasure in us, His children, and when we are meek and full of humility, we become like a company of Josephs, having put on the robe of many colors. When God puts on us the coat of many colors, that beauty is that is given in salvation is embroidered with peace, contentment, joy, holiness, and righteousness.

THE "MAS-SAW" OF THE LORD

When a Christian is restored, they get reconnected with the head and the burden of the Lord is put on them is light. Though the context of this passage speaks about keeping the commandments of the Lord easily, and that you can endure temptations to the end then when you have overcome you will receive the crown of life (see Jam. 1:12) there is another way the burden of Jesus connects to you.

As a prophetic Joseph company made up of prophets and prophetic people the "burden" in Hebrew is "mas-saw." Mas-saw first and foremost is a masculine noun that can be translated in English as "utterance, oracle, burden"[27] or "pronouncement" (New American Standard Bible (NASB)).

GOD CONDEMNS FALSE 'MAS-SAW'S

Before I go on with this topic of "burden of the Lord," I want to want to let you know that there is warning and a judgment on those that give false "pronouncements" or false prophecies or false "burdens" in Jeremiah 23:33-40. Upon review of the context, the following English translations translate "mas-saw" as "burden": Amplified Classic Edition (AMPC), Christian Standard Bible (CSB), English Standard Version (ESV), Holman Christian Standard Bible (HCSB), King James Version (KJV), and the New Revised Standard Version (NRSV).

THE PROPHETIC "MAS-SAW"

Let us look at the teaching of the "burden of the Lord" as the "oracle or pronouncement or message of the Lord," as translated in the

Amplified (AMP), NASB, New International Version, and the New King James Version (NKJV) of the Bible.

The mas-saw in usage in the prophetic sense is given to Zechariah and Malachi. In Zechariah 9:1, 12:1; and Malachi 1:1 in the English Standard Version translates these passages as "The oracle (burden – NKJV) of the word (logos in the Greek Septuagint) of the Lord." When Jesus said that "His burden is light," that as you connect with Him that through the spoken prophetic Word of Jesus that is presented either through a prophet or Scripture draws you in to His light and that Jesus is the light of God.

Another way of saying this is that when we have put Jesus Christ on us the prophetic Word is revelational light to us. It is written that "The spirit of man is Yahweh's lamp, searching all his innermost parts" (Pro. 20:27) and that His word is a lamp to my feet and a light to my path (see Psa. 119:105). This light that He gives is not just His written Word, but also the 5 senses that gives us a deeper dimensional relationship with God. "For the eyes of the Lord are on the righteous, and his ears open to their prayer" (1 Pet. 3:12a).

GET RID OF PRIDE

We, His righteous children, should understand that His gaze is on us. That means He loves us so much that He is constantly looking at us. But, when we sin, "the face of the Lord is against those who do evil" (1 Pet. 3:12a). Yet, "he is faithful and righteous to forgive us the sins, and to cleanse us from all unrighteousness" (1 Joh. 1:9). I encourage you to get pridefulness out of you as the Holy Spirit opens up the seeing realm to you that you do not get prideful.

Above, Wisdom, who is the Lord Jesus Christ, in the *Final Quest Trilogy*, Rick Joyner describes the army of *pride* that is against those that do not wear humility. Wisdom explained, "*It* [pride] *is the hardest enemy to see after you have been in the glory. Those who refuse to put this cloak on will suffer much at the hands of that most devious enemy.*"[28]

Staying Humble (JOSEPH'S ISSUE)

As we dwell in the midst of the Most High God, we must stay humble. For it is written that we are to humble ourselves in the sight of the Lord, and He will lift us up (see Jam. 4:10). To stay humble will save us from many nonessential tribulations. I speak from experience. Please do not let your giftings of seeing and hearing the Spirit, that are part of the Joseph company. Let your life and plans go according to His plan of redemption. Joseph went through many hardships because of his arrogance and pride.

SHARING OUT OF SEASON

Joseph's father rebuked him for the dreams that he shared (see Gen. 37:1-11). There is a time to disclose the prophetic word to people. There is an immaturity in the Body to share things from the Head before the proper time to just get their name(s) out there. Please be careful of the revelations He gives you. Ask for wisdom to send the message(s) out.

As King Solomon wrote that "when pride comes, then comes shame, but with humility comes wisdom" (Pro. 11:2). Then "a man's pride brings him low, but one of lowly spirit gains honor" (Pro. 29:23). Remember that humbleness comes in multiple ways, realms, and experiences. There is the disrespect of the fear of the God's warning. If the warning(s) are not heeded, then comes trials and tribulations. If the lessons are learned, then the reflections of those experiences can be imparted to the generations that need to know the wisdom of God. To have the wisdom of Jesus which is imparted in the Scriptures must be written on and in your hearts.

HUMILITY BRINGS GREATER AUTHORITY

As Joseph grew up, the Lord had mercy or kindness with him to have His will and plan of redemption executed (see Gen. 39:21). As you grow in humility God lifts you up to where He needs you in life. Joseph was given much power and authority over a nation. If you read the Scriptures about God's plan to make him a ruler over much, which is listed below, read it with eyes that reflects our position in Christ Jesus in many different levels of love.

> Pharaoh said to Joseph, "Because God has shown you all of this, there is no one so discreet and wise as you. You shall be over my house. All my people will be ruled according to your word. Only in the throne I will be greater than you." Pharaoh said to Joseph, "Behold, I have set you over all the land of Egypt." Pharaoh took off his signet ring from his hand, and put it on Joseph's hand, and arrayed him in robes of fine linen, and put a gold chain about his neck. He made him ride in the second chariot which he had. They cried before him, "Bow the knee!" He set him over all the land of Egypt. Pharaoh said to Joseph, "I am Pharaoh. Without you, no man shall lift up his hand or his foot in all the land of Egypt" (Gen. 41:39-44).

RULING WITH HUMILITY

Though Pharaoh is seen as the archenemy of Moses and a heathen, there is a type of symbolism where we are to rule over in humility that is given to us through the power of the Lord. It is Jesus who said, "He who overcomes, and he who keeps my works to the end, to him I will give authority over the nations" (Rev. 2:26). As Joseph overcame his tests, he was given the nations. When you pray according to the Father's will, you are given power over the nations.

As Jesus continues to give to us, the Joseph company, who are part of the Army of the Lord, are needed for direction, and will be part of the Overcomers who are "arrayed in white garments, and I will in no way blot his name out of the book of life, and I will confess his name before my Father, and before his angels" (Rev. 3:5). Praise Jesus that He will confess our names before our Father and His holy angels. That is power!

GOD'S SIGNET RING

Joseph was given Pharaoh's signet ring which is what we are given as the "ambassadors on behalf of Christ" (2 Cor. 5:20). Through the Holy Spirit, "—this is the declaration of the Lord of Hosts—'I will take you, Zerubbabel son of Shealtiel, My servant'—this is the Lord's declaration—'and make you like **My signet ring**, for I have chosen you.' This is the declaration of the Lord of Hosts" (Hag. 2:23 HCSB bold mine).

The Lord of all the Heavenly armies addresses the humble that we are to be His signet ring. Not signet rings. But corporately like God is One, so are we, united in love. As Christ's ambassadors we are given a definition of the signet ring from *Got Questions Ministries*:

> Ancient kings used signet rings to designate authority, honor, or ownership. A signet contained an emblem unique to the king. Official documents were sealed with a dollop of soft wax impressed with the king's signet, usually kept on a ring on his finger. Such a seal certified the document as genuine, much like a notary public's stamp today.[29]

Jesus, speaking in a Heavenly Vision to Rick Joyner, in *The Final Quest*:

> I also prayed to My Father on the night before My crucifixion, that the glory I had with Him in the beginning would be with My people, so that you will be one. It is My glory that unifies. As you come together with others who love Me, My glory will be magnified. The more that My glory is magnified by the joining of those who love Me, the more the world will know that I was sent by the Father. Now the world really will know that you are My disciples because you will love Me, and you will love each other.[30]

If you see Jesus's heart in the above passage, the more we get together, the more Jesus's glory is manifested. There is a cloud of glory that fills the physical place of His dwelling. Jesus is saying that we must come together in love towards Him. I will say this, that it is not a lukewarm love, where He will vomit you out of His mouth (see Rev. 3:16), but a passionately driven love. Where you pray for His wisdom on the decisions of the day, and even at that moment.

This Heavenly company of Overcomers will be able, with the Holy Spirit's approval be able to encourage or correct the body in the fashion that is needed. As a people ruled by the Holy Spirit, they will allow God to melt the wax in their life first, and to put His stamp/signet on them. Once that stamp is perfected, He then puts you through the refiner's fire to mold you to the place where you can reflect His nature and bear the seal of His signet ring.

THE GOLDEN CHAIN

Then, Joseph had a gold chain wrapped around his neck. The symbolism of the gold is having the unity of God's nature wrapped around your neck that is touching your very new man nature. This nature is full of God to the point that mercy and truth are bound to your neck and written on the tablet of your hearts (see Pro. 3:3 NKJV) which bears His signet.

BEARING THE SIGNET RING

Like Joseph receiving the authority to rule Egypt, except Pharoah having more authority than Joseph, will be given power to rule over the nations. It is only given to those that are Jesus's Overcoming Body/Church and do the works of Jesus until the very end will this authority be given (see Rev.2:26-27). Jesus will be greater than us because we are to bear His image and we rule only through His authority.

TRUE ADMINISTRATIVE POWER

Joseph was given the power to administrate entrance or removal from the earthly kingdom of Egypt. This authority was given to the Body of Christ in the representation of keys. Jesus, though originally given to Simon Peter, we the Overcomers, that Jesus has given us "the keys of the Kingdom of Heaven, and whatever you bind on earth will have been bound in heaven; and whatever you release on earth will have been released in heaven" (see Mat. 16:18-19). "Elijah was a man with a nature like ours, and he prayed earnestly that it might not rain, and it didn't rain on the earth for three years and six months. He prayed again, and the sky gave rain, and the earth produced its fruit" (Jam. 5:17-18).

Are we going to be able to administrate the kingdom of Heaven on Earth? Are we choosing to administrate binding and loosening without emotional panic and with wisdom? Our praying and administrating justice should be in a humble manner and give place for the Judge to execute our requests based on His judicial system. That He will judge the nations at this time and render the verdicts to those that oppose the will of the Holy Spirit on the Earth.

Again, this must be done in wisdom. Rick Joyner writes in the prophetic vision that Jesus gave him in *The Final Quest* about spiritual authority that is given from Jesus. Jesus says, "the higher the spiritual authority that you walk in, the further you can fall if you are without love and humility.[31]

WALKING IN UNITY AND LOVE

I write to proclaim that the cloak of humility brings unity and love. When you walk in this then walking in humility becomes natural. But you must do things His way, not yours. Though they may seem strange to the natural mind, it is the ways and mind of the Spirit that matters (see Isa. 55:9).

REMEMBER TO INQUIRE TO THE LORD

"For God hath chosen the foolish things of the world to confound the wise" (1 Cor. 1:27a KJV). If you think it is God, and it does not always make sense, test it. I encourage you to try it. If it is of God, inquire to Him about it. In the Old Testament it has been written down since before the Mosaic law was given that people inquired before the Lord. Rebekah, Isaac's wife inquired to the Lord on behalf of Jacob and Esau (see Gen. 25:21-22).

Everywhere else, God spoke to the prophets and the prophets were the ones that inquired to the Lord. It was king Jehoshaphat that spoke "isn't there a prophet of Yahweh here, that we may inquire of Yahweh by him?" (2 Kin. 3:11). In Ezekiel 14:7, Yahweh spoke to the prophet Ezekiel telling him that He will answer the inquiries of the prophets.

It was prophet-priest-king David that wrote that we are to inquire to the Lord (see Psa. 27:4 NKJV) because we live in the glory realms of His temple. Our body is a copy of the Heavenly temple manifested on this Earth. We go into the Holy of Holies when we open our hearts past our feelings, and we begin to know Him. It is through this time in the Word and the Spirit that we grow where He can establish and enlarge the mantle/cloak of humility. This cloak allows you to fully operate in the five-dimensional senses of the Spirit.

BEING CLOTHED WITH HUMILITY PART 1

Holy Spirit in the name of Jesus I put on and sink into the clothing of humility. I thank you for showing me that this cloak goes over every garment that is upon my body. I ask that you keep me humble and that I can inquire into Your temple through the Holy Spirit every moment of my life. Like David, I want to be able to gaze at the beauty of Your holiness. Let me have the ability to walk in the unity of the Spirit and "agapao" love that Jesus requires of me. Amen.

Chapter 10: Clothed With Humility (Part 2 – The Eyes of the Spirit)

THE DIMENSIONAL SENSE of Seeing (THE eyes)

I want to reiterate the reason for humility in the Generation "ZION" of Seers. Rick Joyner in *The Final Quest* describes what happens when you are clothed in humility.

> I could not make out what I was seeing because the glory shining from my armor made it difficult to see into the darkness. I asked Wisdom if there was something that I could cover my armor with so I could see it. He then gave me a very plain mantel to put on.
>
> "What is this?" I inquired, a little insulted by its drabness.
>
> "*Humility*," said Wisdom. "*You will not be able to see very well without it.*"
>
> Reluctantly I put it on, and immediately I saw many things that I could not see before.[32]

As you embark on the prophet's mantle of seeing that you remain humble. As a Seer, you will see things that you have not seen before. To be a true Seer, there must be Heavenly encounters. When you start seeing, you will have Holy Spirit encounters. The Spirit encounters of the Seer are not limited to angelic, but those encounters should be of our risen Lord Jesus Christ, and others that can see into the demonic realm for battle plans that are need for fighting against the satanic kingdom. A true Seer sees first because of the uses of sight.

James W. Goll in *The Seer* describes 12 expressions or variations of the prophetic ministries of the Holy Spirit:

1. Dreamers and Visionaries.

1. Prophets Who Proclaim God's Corporate Purpose.

1. Prophets Who Proclaim God's Heart Standards for His People.

1. Prophets Who Proclaim the Church's Social Responsibilities and Actions.

1. Prophets Who Speak Forth the Administrative Strategy of God With a Political Slant.

1. Prophetic Worship Leaders Who Usher in the Manifested Presence of God Through Prophetic Worship.

1. Prophetic Intercessors.

1. Spirit-Bearers.

1. Prophetic Counselors.

1. Prophetic Equippers.

1. Prophetic Writers.

1. Prophetic Evangelists.[33]

Within these expressions there is an aspect of seeing that will relate to the other senses of the Spirit that require humility. As a prophetic writer, I challenge you that you study God's Word, and encourage you to read Jim W. Goll's book on *The Seer*. The Holy Spirit gives you a message no matter what it is that must be given. Sometimes this gift of seeing is only meant to be used in intercession or spoken to an individual that will be used to exemplify Jesus, and Jesus only.

The Seer dimension must have a revelatory gifting. The revelation is not something new, but an aspect of bringing Heaven to Earth. As Jim W. Goll in *The Seer*, writes that you must seek a vision that sustains you.[34]

VISIONARY STATES (PART 1)

The first four of eight Greek words used to describe the type of visionary states that Christians may experience are given briefly by Jim W. Goll in *The Seer*:

1. *Onar* is the common word for "dream." This is the normal dreaming everyone does. Biblical examples are (Mat. 1:20, 24-25; Mat. 2:12-14; Mat. 2:19-21; Mat. 27:19).[35]

1. *Enupnion* is when you receive a vision or dream you receive in your sleep that emphasizes a surprised quality of expression in the dream. Biblical examples are (Jud. 8-9; Act. 2:17).[36]

1. *Horama* is "another general term for vision" or to literally "that which is seen." They are *waking visions* that carry "the particular sense of a 'spectacle, sight, or appearance." Biblical examples are (Mat. 17:9; Act. 9:10-12; Act. 10:3-4; Act. 10:19-20; Act. 16:9-10; Act. 18:9-11).[37]

1. *Horasis* is used very little in the New Testament. The meaning of it does not distinguish between the physical and spiritual eyes. The "seeing" is regarded as genuine perception externally and internally. When we "see" in the spiritual realm or dimensions we "see with the eyes of our heart" (see Eph. 1:18). Our eyes are the "windows" where the Holy Spirit likes to look through because we are the His temple.[38] A different way to phrase this example is when the Holy Spirit "looks out through the 'windows' of our eyes and allows to see what He sees."[39] There are times that we see *both* spiritually and physically overlapping each other. You see in the natural, but you see a dual vision spiritually superimposed over the physical eyesight.[40]

ADAM'S ORIGINAL HORASIS

In the Greek Old Testament called The Septuagint or LXX, the word "horasis", most of the time is translated in English as vision. The Strong's concordance defines it as "the act of gazing, i.e. (externally) an aspect or (internally) an inspired appearance:—sight, vision."[41] This is the same word that is used in Acts 2:17, which is the quote of Joel 2:28 from the LXX, which states:

It will happen afterward, that I will pour out my Spirit on all flesh; and your sons and your daughters will prophesy. Your old men will dream dreams. Your young men will see visions [*horasis*].

Looking deeper into *horasis* and the Septuagint, the Greek Old Testament, the word *horasis* is first given in Genesis 2:9. "Out of the ground Yahweh God made every tree to grow that is pleasant to the sight [*horasis*], and good for food, including the tree of life in the middle of the garden and the tree of the knowledge of good and evil."

In context of the preliminary verses God had formed Adam but had not yet formed Eve or been taken out of Adam's side or formed from Adam's rib. God brought and placed Adam in the Garden of Eden (see Gen. 2:7-8). Adam's job was to tend the garden and commanded to eat of every tree except the tree of knowledge of good and evil with the consequence of death (see Gen. 2:15-17).

It has been God's purpose for us to be able to see in the Spirit realm while seeing in the natural since the age of first tending the Garden in Eden. Every tree was given for food and that it was pleasant to look at physically. We were created to be a people of visions (*horasis*). It was in this state that God was able to commune with Adam with no limitations. He was partnering with Adam in letting him name the creatures that were formed from the dust of the Earth and the birds of the air (see Gen.2:19).

ADAM VS JESUS

Taking Scripture in context of the difference between Adam and Jesus, the last Adam, we should note that and logically deduce that the Holy Spirit lived in Adam, as the breath of life (see Gen. 2:7) that was given to him. Jesus was the "child of the Holy Spirit" (see Mat. 1:18 RSV) and we like Jesus are children of God for "the Spirit himself testifies with our spirit that we are children of God" (Rom. 8:16). Jesus discussing with Nicodemus that those who are born of the Spirit are born again are spiritually born and are part of the Son of Man who comes from heaven (see Joh. 3:5-17). Then that makes Adam as a child of God born of the natural and born of the Spirit.

Knowing that to have visions and "see in the Spirit" should be natural since this commenced at the Day of Pentecost. The Holy Spirit was given to "receive power when the Holy Spirit has come upon you. You will be witnesses to me in Jerusalem, in all Judea and Samaria, and to the uttermost parts of the earth" (Act. 1:8) to fulfill this commission.

We now understand that to see in the Spirit is seeing with the eyes of the heart that was originally given to Adam and is fulfilled by Jesus through the Holy Spirit that we are living in the Spiritual realm of God's Garden.

SEEING WITH HUMILITY AND GRACE

For in humility and grace we see have our eyes opened to the things of the Spirit. We are given grace for it is written in Isaiah 51:3 that:

> For Yahweh has comforted Zion. He has comforted all her waste places, and has made her wilderness like Eden, and her desert like the garden of Yahweh. Joy and gladness will be found in them, thanksgiving, and the voice of melody.

GLIMPSES OF WHAT THE FATHER AND SON SEE

As we stay humble about being able to have sight [*horasis*] without limit or measure, feeling humble about this honor to see the Supernatural through the Spirit's eyes is amazing. Imagine it like this, that the Father and Jesus are giving you glimpses of what they see through the Holy Spirit and giving you a perception of the mind of Christ (see 1 Cor. 2:16). When we receive this, it is the Holy Spirit watering our seeing dimension to grow with greater fruit to help the body become pure without any spots or wrinkles (see Eph. 5:27).

mar-eh' with horasis

In the Hebrew the word for sight is *mar-eh'* which is a masculine noun and then we have *horasis* which is a feminine noun. Therefore, showing us that the Bridegroom, who is Jesus Christ, is the one that intends for us to have sight [mar-eh] (masculine) and we the Bride of Christ are to receive that sight [horasis] (feminine).

THE TREE OF LIFE BRINGS PRODUCES HORASIS

Going back to Adam in Eden and when he was instructed that "out of the ground Yahweh God made every tree to grow that is pleasant to the sight, and good for food..." (Gen. 2:9). The trees were then given for us to see and were good for eating. Proceeding further, Genesis advises that "...the tree of life in the middle of the garden and the tree of the knowledge of good and evil" (Gen. 2:9).

The tree of life gave birth to all the fruit. When we are told that the fruit was "pleasant to the sight" (see Gen. 2:9a) The phrase "pleasant to" is the Hebrew word *khaw-mad* can also be translated to "desire."[42] Another rendering of this phrase in view of desiring spiritual gifts, but "especially that you may prophesy" (1 Cor. 14:1) that we are to desire to have visions [horasis] where that desire is derived from the center of the Garden of God, the tree of life.

GOD – THE TRUE TREE OF LIFE

The tree of life is meant to give us eternal life physically and has healing properties. Jesus is the one that leads us to the tree of life. God is the true tree of life for in Him is true life through Jesus Christ. We are told that we will eat of the fruit of the tree of life that is in the middle of God's paradise on Mount Zion (see Rev. 2:7).

THE TREE OF LIFE'S FRUIT

The tree of life gives twelve fruits a year which is the middle of the street of the New Jerusalem and along the river of life (see Rev. 21:10; Rev. 22:1-2). This shows the tree of life replicates itself. The fruit of the tree of life gives multiple fruits. We partake of the fruit of the tree of life for its fruit will allow us to have more visions as we desire it.

Jesus is connected to the tree of life because as a grapevine and we are connected to Him. As His branches we must bear fruit (see Joh. 15:5). This fruit that we bear is all produced through the Holy Spirit. The fruit of the Spirit are "love, joy (gladness), peace, patience (an even temper, forbearance), kindness, goodness (benevolence), faithfulness, gentleness (meekness, humility), self-control (self-restraint, continence)" (Gal. 5:22-23a AMPC), goodness, righteousness, and truth (Eph. 5:9). Goodness is a double portion fruit.

THE DOUBLE PORTION FRUIT

Like Elisha asking for a double portion of Elijah's spirit (see 2 Kin. 2:9) and because we are the priests of the Yahweh and are called God's servants, we either have been in one way or another tortured, ridiculed, robbed, etc. For our faithfulness and enduring shame, Jesus will give us double honor (see Isa. 61:6-7). It is that double portion of the Holy Spirit that we are given as a foretaste, but we are given the spirit without measure (see Joh. 3:34).

As our "weeping prophet" brother Jeremiah, writing about the restoration of natural Jerusalem we are told in Jeremiah 33:9 that:

> This city [Jerusalem] will be to me for a name of joy, for praise, and for glory, before all the nations of the earth, which will hear all the good that I do to them, and will fear and tremble for all the good and for all the peace that I provide to it.

As natural Jerusalem will be a name of joy, a praise, and honor to God and all the nations of the Earth because of everything that God does for them is good. This applies to Spiritual Jerusalem, us, who are partakers of a time coming and yet realize that the fruit we receive is honor before all the nations because of the goodness God gives us through Jesus Christ and the result of that honor and goodness is prosperity. Prosperity beyond riches of natural monetary gain, which includes that, but also spiritual monetary gain. We are to store our treasures in our spiritual heavenly treasure box because that is where our heart should be (see Mat. 6:20-21).

Through our praising of Jesus by giving us the honor of seeing our enemies gathered before us knowing they fear and tremble at God is where we must remain humble. This praise we give him is based on the *garment of praise* we have been given and clothed in. We sing, dance, clap our hands, rejoice in all ways that are appropriate to Him which are not mundane and dry but lovely expressions of our heart's desire to Him.

VISIONS BEAR EDIFICATION

As we desire to have visions, where the treasures of where the usage of the victories of the visions are stored must bear fruit for the edification of the Body of Christ for God to keep giving them to us. Jane Hamon wrote in the book *Discernment* about operating with "Holy Spirit radar" the following:

> God has given every believer the supernatural ability to operate with "Holy Spirit radar" to see and sense things in the unseen realm. John 7:24 tells us to "look beneath the surface so you can judge correctly" (New Living Translation). Hidden things are revealed so the Church can come to a greater place of authority, health and liberty; it is possible even for regions in the earth to be set free.[43]

We must mature and understand that the horasis (visions) are not for private understanding but must be interpreted in light of Scripture (see 2 Pet. 1:20). Through humility, respect, and honor to the Holy Spirit who gives us them we ought to know that He will give horasis (visions) in abundance if we keep on desiring to see and eat from the fruit of the Spirit.

ABUNDANT LIFE

Hamon wrote in the book *Discernment* on abundance the following that Jesus commented on about abundance:

> Jesus says, "The thief comes only in order to steal and kill and destroy. I came that they may have and enjoy life and have it in abundance (to the full, until it overflows)" (see John 10:10b AMP). The Greek word for *abundant life* means "superabundant in quantity, superior to quality, exceeding, abundant above, beyond measure, more, more eminent, more remarkable, more excellent, more than necessary, super-added."[44]

When we live in abundance, we live in the glory realm where nothing can shake us. To live there brings peace through any storm you face. The Great I AM is with you. The one who we cast our cares upon misses you if you do not rely on Him. For He will let you eat of the tree of life when you have overcome challenges (see Rev. 2:7).

THE TWO TREES

That is why the tree of life is mentioned as the first of the two trees in Genesis 2:9. The reason the tree of knowledge is given as the second tree is that it identifies the dark demonic realm that twists things and is under control of the soulish realm. For in the soulish realm is where the serpent hides itself and lives (see Gen. 3:1-10).

It is in this realm where words are twisted to either lies or half-truths. Truth is mingled with death. This is the realm that the non-Christian starts life. When the Holy Spirit lives in the Christian they can begin partaking of the tree of life. But the tree of knowledge of good and evil must be dealt with and have its fruit cut off and that tree burned. It is in this dark demonic/satanic realm where psychics, false priests, heathen, and the lusts of the flesh come from. This is inherited from the original Adam.

RESTORATION OF ALL WORDS OF SEERS

Once the truth has been given and we are restored to the operation of what we originally were given as seers of the Holy Spirit, we can move forward in understanding the rest of the terms of the different aspects of "seeing."

VISIONARY STATES (PART 2)

The remaining four of the eight Greek words used to describe the type of visionary states that Christian experiences are given by Jim W. Goll in *The Seer*:

1. *Optasia* is "visuality" in concrete form, apparition. Biblical examples are (Luk. 1:22; Luk. 24:22-23; 2 Cor. 12:1-4).[45]

1. *Ekstasis* is where the English word "ecstasy" is derived...determining its usage it can be translated means "amazement, astonishment, or a trance. Literally, *ekstatis*

means 'a displacement of the mind,' or 'bewilderment.' When translated as 'trance,' *ekstasis* refers to one being caught up in the Spirit so as to receive those revelations that God intends. This is very likely the state that John was referring to in Revelation 1:10 when he wrote, 'I was in the Spirit on the Lord's day, and I heard behind me a loud voice like the sound of a trumpet.'" Biblical examples are (Luk. 5:26; Act 3:9-10; Mrk 16:8; Act 22:17-18).[46]

1. *Apokalupsis* is the common word for the description of a "visionary state." It "literally means 'disclosure,' an 'appearing or coming,' a 'manifestation.'"[47]

The 18 biblical examples are (Luk. 2;32; Rom. 2:5; Rom. 8:19; Rom. 16:25; 1 Cor. 1:7; 1 Cor. 14:6; 1 Cor. 14:26; 2 Cor. 12:1; 2 Cor. 12:7; Gal. 1:12; Gal. 2:2; Eph. 1:17; Eph. 3:3; 2 Th. 1:7; 1 Pet. 1:7; 1 Pet. 1:13; 1 Pet. 4:13; Rev. 1:1).

1. *Egenomehn Ehn Pneumati* is a phrase that literally means "to *become* in the Spirit."[48]

It is a state in which one could see visions and be informed or spoken directly to by the Spirit of God. Therein lies the secret to how we get revelation. How do we receive insight? How do we see visions? We do it by getting in the Spirit. The more we are filled with the Spirit and walk in the Spirit, the more we become one with the Spirit, and the more our eyes will be opened to see in the Spirit. He will give us the perception to look into the spiritual realm.[49]

BEING CLOTHED WITH HUMILITY PART 2

Holy Spirit in the name of Jesus I put on and sink into the clothing of humility with the aspect of seeing in the Spirit. As you open my eyes to see according to the original *horasis*, I ask that you provide me with the perfect manifestation of seeing according to Your will in my life. Amen.

Chapter 11: Clothed With Humility (Part 3 – The Ears of the Spirit)

THE DIMENSIONAL SENSE of hearing (THE ears)

James W. Goll in *The Coming Prophetic Revolution* lists 20 ways on how God speaks to us, though this list is not all encompassing:

> As a good carpenter has more than one tool in his tool chest, so we must have a good assortment of tools available to us in order to properly build the house of the Lord. Here are a few scriptural examples that portray the diversity of tools the Spirit uses to speak to people:

1. A dream or vision (see Job 33:14-18).

1. A voice in a trance (see Acts 10:9-16).

1. The voice of many angels (see Rev. 5:11).

1. The voice of the archangel (see 1 Thess. 4:16).

1. The "sound of many waters" (Rev. 1:15).

1. The sound of the Lord walking in the Garden (see Gen. 3:8).

1. The sound of the army of God marching in the tops of the trees (see 2 Sam. 5:23-25).

1. The audible voice of God (see Exod. 3:4).

1. God "speaking peace" to His people (Ps. 85:8).

1. God's written Word (our primary source of His voice and our chief reference point).

1. Wonders in the sky and on Earth (see Joel 2:30-31).

1. Visions and parables to the prophets (see Hosea 12:10).

1. Words and physical metaphors to the prophets (see Jer. 18:1-6).

1. The Holy Spirit speaking to a group (see Acts 13:2).

1. Men, moved by the Holy Spirit, declaring God's voice (see 2 Pet. 1:21).

1. Heavenly experiences in which one is brought up before the Lord (see 2 Cor. 12:1-4).

1. The Holy Spirit bearing witness to our spirit (see Rom. 8:16).

1. A dumb donkey speaking with the voice of a man (see 2 Pet. 2:16).

1. One person speaking the revelatory counsel of the Lord to another (see Jas. 5:19-20).

1. God's own Son (see Heb. 1:2).[50]

The Dimensional Sense of Hearing (ears)

As you continue to listen to God's voice there are 10 principles of Divine guidance that James W. Goll gives in *The Beginner's Guide to Hearing God*: [51]

1. The Will of God Is Made Known in the Word of God.

1. The Will of God Is Confirmed Through Circumstances.

1. The Holy Spirit Speaks from Where He Dwells.

1. Divine Guidance Comes from Meeting God's Conditions.

1. Peace of God Accompanies True Guidance.

1. Much Guidance from God Comes Unnoticed.

1. Divine Guidance Does Not Mean We Know All the Details.

1. The Process of Guidance Is Not Always Pleasant.

1. Hearing God Speak Should Prompt Us to Action.

1. Guidance Is a Skill to Be Learned over a Lifetime.

As you continue to hear God's voice, I encourage to stay humble to not have your will but God's will. That your prayers are not hindered because of arrogance from hearing God's voice.

BEING CLOTHED WITH HUMILITY PART 3

Holy Spirit in the name of Jesus I put on and sink into the clothing of humility with the aspect of hearing/listening in the Spirit. As you open my ears to hear/listen I ask that you provide me with the grace to guide me to listen and understand according to Your will in my life. Amen.

Chapter 12: Clothed With Humility (Part 4 – Feeling/Touching in the Spirit)

THE DIMENSIONAL SENSE of touching (THE hands/feet)

The Hands of Healing

The sensory realm of touch is presented in a positive aspect from Jesus. It is called the doctrine of laying on of hands (see Heb. 6:2). It is the five-fold ministry where the pinky is the teacher. The ring-finger is the pastor who is married to the congregation. The middle finger is the evangelist who proclaims the good news of Jesus Christ. The index finger is the prophet who points the way back to God with a specific message that the Holy Spirit has laid upon the heart. The thumb is the apostle who operates like a father, influencing all the other ministries, and can work in conjunction with the other four fingers or gifts from Jesus Christ.

In Scripture, God the Father could not physically touch humans because of the sinful flesh of man. But when Jesus came forward in the name of Yahweh that by His touch people were healed (see Mat. 9:20-22; Mat. 14:35-36; Mar. 5:25-34; Mar. 6:56; Luk. 8:43-48). He was also resurrected from the realm of death (see Mat. 9:23-25; Mar. 5:35-42; Luk. 8:49-56).

It is God the Father in these last days that draws people to Jesus and allows them to spiritually feel His touch through the Holy Spirit. But it is through human hands that we co-labor in reaching those that need healing of the natural and spiritual body. When we lay hands on people, it is this initial touch that people receive the Holy Spirit's touch. The more prayed up and submitted to God in your life the more the Holy Spirit can use you. The anointing that flows from your hands. This anointing is described in Habakkuk 3:4 (CJB) where it is written that "rays come forth from His hand - that is where His power is concealed." As previously written, the Holy Spirit's power is designed for, and is used for healing of the five natural/spiritual senses.

THE FEET OF DOMINION

The feet and dominion ministry of Jesus Christ is not limited to just evangelism but also for taking back land in the spirit realm that the Holy Spirit does not yet occupy. The Holy Spirit is the one that moves on behalf of Jesus during the Warrior Bridal age. This is where we commune in battle as a unit and move like one man (see Jdg. 6:16). We do not move as a lone ranger but as a corporate body because Jesus said that He is there where two or three are gathered in His name He is there (see Mat. 18:20). We are taking back dominion that Jesus has already won, though there is a battle. We can face it, endure it, and overcome it. We are a company of Overcomers that honor the eternal dominion of Jesus Christ now and forever (see 1 Pet. 4:11; 1 Pet. 5:11; Jud. 1:25; Rev. 1:6).

BEING CLOTHED WITH HUMILITY PART 4

Holy Spirit in the name of Jesus I put on and sink into the clothing of humility with the aspect of my hands and feet would be filled with healing and dominion in the Spirit. As you charge me with the commission to take authority in different realms, I ask that Your anointing flow through me because Your Holy Spirit touches me. Let that touch be pure and holy. Let the rainbow light of life flow through my hands and help those that are physically, spiritually, mentally, and emotionally bound get set free. Amen.

Chapter 13: Clothed With Humility (Part 5 – The Aroma of the Spirit)

THE DIMENSIONAL SENSE of Smelling (THE NOSE)

When you think about aroma and sweet-smelling fragrances, what do you think about? The description of the Shulamite's garments is like the "fragrance of Lebanon" (see Son. 4:11d-e AMP). The Shulamite is a type of the Bride of Christ. Let us look at it from the *Šôʿēriym* wardrobe point of view.

The fragrance is a reference to cedar and hyssop.[52] The cedar fragrance repels snakes, and the hyssop is a spiritual cleanser that the Levitical priests used. They would dip the hyssop in the blood of a lamb and sprinkle it on the person. We as Christians have been washed in the blood of the Lamb of God and we are pure. The hyssop is a plant that reminds of cleansing and sacrifice. It has a minty smell to it because it is part of the mint family.

THE AROMA OF LIFE OR DEATH

As we are clothed in humility its fragrance is used to keep us pure through not seeking our will but the will of the One who entrusted us to take His message to the nations. This clothing that is worn shows our relationship "for we are a sweet aroma of Christ to God, in those who are saved and in those who perish: to the one a stench from death to death, to the other a sweet aroma from life to life" (2 Cor. 2:15-16).

We are to "walk in love, even as Christ also loved us and gave himself up for us, an offering and a sacrifice to God for a sweet-smelling fragrance" (Eph. 5:2). When we have humility on, we are showing that as we sacrifice ourselves in submission to the Holy Spirit because Christ died in our place and became the sweet-smelling aroma to God. That is the aroma that leads to life and when the enemies of God which are in the world system sees us, the aroma smells horrible to them.

This submission is anything that keeps us from the knowledge of the Holy One. It is the knowledge of grace, mercy, and love that in Christ is revealed through us to the world. We are the light that Jesus has commanded to be with a sweet-smelling aroma or fragrance which are the prayers sent to God as incense (see Rev. 5:8).

THE TANGIBLE AROMA

The aroma of the Holy Spirit is also tangible. As a witness to this awesome aroma, it is compared to the clean smell that happens after it has rained or to me it can be like the rose of Sharon or lilies. The rose of Sharon is what is known as Hibiscus trees and is a mild sweet smell that to me is intoxicating with a desire to love Jesus more.

My daughter Sharlotte is sensitive to the aroma of God's presence. At the time of this writing she is a preteen, with the description of this manifestation that can first be smelled, felt, then seen. Sharlotte's encounter of the aroma as she describes it as "sweet as French Vanilla."

One of her favorite flavors is French vanilla. When she smells the Holy Spirit, it is like a love that is intoxicating to her that she can sense peace, excitement, and joy. When He comes in and she is playing in His presence, she giggles more than ever.

Those fragrances, especially the rose of Sharon, prepare me for what is going to happen next. It is a wake-up scent that when known allows the Holy Spirit to move in the direction He chooses. The aroma is manifested through cultivation of the Holy Spirit. The Spirit of prophecy, when allowed to move, will manifest Himself to those that are sensitive in the Spirit.

PRAYER RELEASES THE AROMA

The aroma of the Lord is God's answered reciprocation of prayers, worship, praise, declarations, and intercession which are the prayers of the saints. Jim W. Goll gives a great teaching of intercession in his book, *The Lost Art of Intercession*. There are some passages that I will quote from Jim's book that I believe will help you understand the sweet-smelling aroma of Ephesians 5:2.

Jim W. Goll in *The Lost Art of Intercession* writes:

> the Presence of God always descended *after* the fragrance of prayer ascended... An entire kingdom of priests has been authorized and commissioned to minister in God's Presence, offering up unceasing prayer, praise, worship, and intercession for all men.[53]

INTERACTING WITH GOD THROUGH PRAYER

We are to be like David that we are to literally sit before God's presence. This is not something that should be special to the Believer. They get to spend time with their dad. Remember it takes a special person to be a dad or Abba. An Abba is interactive with His family. Our true Abba interacts with us. My question to you is, are you interacting back with Him? That interaction is prayer. Prayer is more than being on your knees, it is praying in many ways, shapes, and forms. But it also lies prostrate before the King, if possible.

THE AROMA IS BUILT UPON A HABITATION

The aroma is built upon making a habitation for the Lord. Briefly written, this subject of the glory cloud follows intense and extravagant worship and intercession. The Holy Spirit wants to have a place of continual habitation that is based upon the "a house of prayer for all nations" (Mar. 11:17) model.

As a House of Prayer for all Nations is being built in the Spirit realm of corporate believers that we are called as the Church of the New Testament of the risen Messiah Jesus. This is why we all need to go to the Father's Throne of Grace with the ability to continually offer worship, praise, and prayer.

PRAYER FOR THE LOST AND BACKSLIDERS

Are the garments you wear seamlessly worn together to worship, pray, and intercede by standing in the gap? I ask you to mediate, pray, intercede by standing in the gap for the lost or backslider by proclaiming this prayer:

I pray to You God that as You send me or someone else to anyone that does not know your goodness or a backslider that You "open their [spiritual] eyes so that they may turn from darkness to light and from the power of Satan to God, that they may receive forgiveness *and* release from their sins and an inheritance among those who have been sanctified (set apart, made holy) by faith in Me" (Act. 26:18 AMP).

PRAYERS TO REMOVE THE STENCHES OF SIN

We can also pray a prayer for us praying:

Lord touch us, let us smell Your sweet aroma. Touch us Your people. As You touch us with the Divine aroma, I also pray that You, Holy Spirit, take away the stench of sin that fills the nostrils of any sinner or backslider with a fresh wind of love, mercy, and grace to fill their/our nostrils with Your sweet aroma and fill their hearts with Your love, Oh Lord!

BEING CLOTHED WITH HUMILITY PART 5

Holy Spirit in the name of Jesus I put on and sink into the clothing of humility with the aspect having Your sweet aroma/fragrance fill my nostrils. Lord, I pray for the fresh wind of love, mercy, and grace to fill my heart. Let me feel the beat of Your heart in my heart. Let it be of true Divine love that I reciprocate towards You through humility then to humanity. Amen.

Chapter 14: Clothed With Humility (Part 6 – Tasting in the Spirit)

THE DIMENSIONAL SENSE of Tasting (The Tongue)

As tasting is a natural sense that God gave us, it must also be true in the realm of the Spirit. David wrote "Oh taste and see that Yahweh is good. Blessed is the man who takes refuge in him" (Psa. 34:8). You see when we know how good the Lord Jesus is to us that we can taste it in our mouth spiritually. Tasting the presence of the Lord is an element of enjoyment that is pleasing to the mouth.

This phrase is also saying that as we who trust in God, we are blessed to know that He looks after us by understanding that we are not lacking. Jesus is life to those that are willing to eat and drink of His Spirit. Jesus proclaimed to be the bread of life (see Joh. 6:35) and declared that when we drink of the water that we receive from Him, we will not thirst again (see Joh. 4:14).

THE WORD IS HONEY TO OUR LIPS

It is written "how sweet are your promises to my taste, more than honey to my mouth!" (Psa. 119:103). The Word of God is sweet to our lips. It is what gives us our spiritual nourishment. Reading, hearing, and obeying are the key aspects of having His Word become sweeter than honey in our mouths.

Solomon was acquainted with this Hebraic thought about Scripture being sweet and life to a person's life. Our lives should reflect our spiritual and natural bodies as one continuous life and not separate from those parts of our bodies. We as children of God, the Holy Spirit writes to us that He instructs by saying "My son, eat honey, for it is good, the droppings of the honeycomb, which are sweet to your taste" (Pro. 24:13). Solomon goes on to state that "pleasant words are a honeycomb, sweet to the soul, and health to the bones" (Pro. 16:24).

It is in the honeycomb that a beekeeper extracts the sweet honey that helps our soul and keeps our bones healthy which again is symbolically interpreted as God's Word to our lives. The prophet Ezekiel testifies about a Theophany or the Father's instructions to him that "He said to me, 'Son of man, eat what you find. <u>Eat this scroll, and go, speak to the house of Israel</u>.' So I opened my mouth, and he caused me to eat the scroll. He said to me, '<u>Son of man, cause your belly to eat, and fill your bowels with this scroll that I give you</u>.' Then I ate it; and <u>it was as sweet as honey in my mouth</u>" (Eze. 3:1-3, underline mine).

If you notice that the scroll is a reference to multiple aspects of our history as Christians. First, the Old Testament was written on scrolls of sheep, calves, and goats. The scrolls of God's Word are written on the scrolls of our heart and sealed with the love of God in Christ Jesus's blood at the Cross.

THE MILK OF THE WORD

The Word of God is also described as milk that we are to desire when we are babies in the Lord to grow in maturity to solid Christians. This pure milk that we have tasted is the Lord's graciousness or unmerited favor (see 1 Pet. 2:2-3). This milk that is given is only for the spiritually immature and "not experienced in the word of righteousness" (Heb. 5:13b). The milk of the Scriptures are the basic doctrines/foundations of the Bible. They are "repentance from dead works, of faith toward God, of the teaching of baptisms, of laying on of hands, of resurrection of the dead, and of eternal judgment" (Heb. 6:1b-2).

THE SOLID WORD FOR THE MATURE

We are also told that we are to eat or taste in maturity solid food. "But solid food is for those who are full grown, who by reason of use have their senses exercised to discern good and evil" (Heb. 5:14). As you mature, God gives you perception on the development of all your senses. It is with these senses in the Spirit realm that discernment is learned, authorized, and applied to recognize and identify good and evil for the ability to edify the Body. This is solid food which is known as "meat" in 1 Corinthians 3:2.

THE LEAVENED BREAD OF FALSE DOCTRINES

Another element of tasting is unleavened bread. The last supper was taken at Passover or called the feast of unleavened bread (see Luk. 22:1). It was this type of bread that the apostles ate with Jesus. When we partake of communion, we are celebrating Jesus's last meal and partaking of the "feast of unleavened bread."

Unleavened bread is bread that is not mixed with leaven or yeast. For when leaven is added to bread it makes it rise. Jesus taught the leaven from the Pharisees is hypocrisy (see Luk. 12:1).

He also warned about watching out of false doctrines or teachings that the Pharisees and Sadducees gave (see Mat. 16:5, 12). Meaning that there are teachings that teach God's truth that it is mingled with errors. They gave religious rules that they did not follow. Some will add or subtract from the teachings of Jesus. Some will say Jesus plus this or that. I will reiterate that it is Jesus plus nothing. Jesus is the way, the truth, and the life (see Joh. 14:6a). Let us be true to the living unleavened Bread.

PURGE THE LEAVEN

Paul tells us to expel all forms of immorality and arrogance in our lives and not to keep company with people like that. That is the leaven that is spoken of in the passage of 1 Corinthians 5:1-2. He goes on to say to "purge out the old yeast, that you may be a new lump, even as you are unleavened. For indeed Christ, our Passover, has been sacrificed in our place. Therefore let's keep the feast, not with old yeast, neither with the yeast of malice and wickedness, but with the unleavened bread of sincerity and truth" (1 Cor. 5:7-8).

This unleavened bread is to the sacrifice that we purge our lives by confessing sin, embracing forgiveness, and not revisiting those sins again. As the Passover meal was a symbol is Jesus's death and resurrection for curing the sin problem that humanity inherited from Adam. The Passover originally could cover the sins temporarily but had to be done yearly where Jesus finalized it by offering His life.

> For concerning those who were once enlightened and tasted of the heavenly gift, and were made partakers of the Holy Spirit, and tasted the good word of God and the powers of the age to come, and then fell away, it is impossible to renew them again to repentance; seeing they crucify the Son of God for themselves again, and put him to open shame (Heb. 6:4-6).

GIDEON, MEAT, AND UNLEAVEND BREAD

There is a passage in Scripture where Gideon interacts the Angel of the Lord or Yahweh or also called the Angel of God, which is a Christophany, or an Old Testament appearance of Jesus Christ in Judges 6:11-25. Let us review versus 20 and 21 specifically.

> The angel of God said to him, "Take the meat and the unleavened cakes, and lay them on this rock, and pour out the broth." He did so. Then Yahweh's angel stretched out the end of the staff that was in his hand, and touched the meat and the unleavened cakes; and fire went up out of the rock and consumed the meat and the unleavened cakes. Then Yahweh's angel departed out of his sight.

Please note that it was goat meat and unleavened bread that was laid on a specific rock and was consumed by fire. This symbolizes that when we mature, we lay down everything that we know and anything that entangles us to things of this world, which are contrary to the

Scriptures, at the feet of Jesus. The broth symbolizes the comingling nutrients of false thinking that go along the digestive track. That is the bitterness of death which is dumped out. This type of thinking produces a form of false humility, pride, malice, wickedness, and/or arrogance.

As Jesus receives and accepts this sacrifice of the goat meat and the unleavened bread in our lives, His fire of acceptance burns out that leaven and the goat style of thinking, which is put under His feet and then under our feet. This symbolizes that it is dealt with and that "it is finished" (Joh. 19:30).

THE WATER WITH NO THIRST

We also taste by drinking water. Earlier it was written that Jesus gives us water where we will not thirst again (see Joh. 4:14). This water comes from God's throne as a river of life that is given by the Spirit and the bride (see Rev. 22:1, 17). This water is described as clear as crystal. This river is cool, which refreshes us for we are in times or seasons of refreshing (see Act. 3:19b). As we get refreshed, we know that when we are spiritually parched the Holy Spirit hydrates us.

This hydration brings our body into alignment with His will and allows us to become fully hydrated in the Holy Spirit. The river is also symbolic of the Holy Spirit. The Holy Spirit also correlates that He is being sent from the Father's throne to revive us into a right relationship with the Father. It is in this relationship that our cup starts to get filled then starts to overflow. Through the overflow we then start to manifest the power of the Holy Spirit.

INVITATION FOR AN ABUNDANT LIFE

When we manifest the power of the Holy Spirit this is when Jesus turns the water to wine (see Joh. 2:9; Joh. 4:46) is what happens when we are in overflow mode. It is this new wine that is manifested on the mountains (see Joe. 3:18a-b) to give Jesus Christ all glory.

Abba is extending the offering to have our taste senses opened up and used for His glory. Let this materialize in your life and make it a reality. For He invites you to eat and drink with Him. This invitation to have an abundant life that Jesus provides to you.

COME EAT AND DRINK IN ABUNDANCE

As God was merciful to king David, so will He also be merciful to you. This is what the Spirit and the Bride invite you to participate in which is provided to us through the River of Life and the Bread of Life. This Word of invitation is given in Isaiah 55:1-3:

Hey! Come, everyone who thirsts, to the waters!

Come, he who has no money, buy, and eat!

Yes, come, buy wine and milk without money and without price.

Why do you spend money for that which is not bread, and your labor for that which doesn't satisfy?

Listen diligently to me, and eat that which is good, and let your soul delight itself in richness.

Turn your ear, and come to me.

Hear, and your soul will live.

I will make an everlasting covenant with you, even the sure mercies of David.

BEING CLOTHED WITH HUMILITY PART 6

Holy Spirit in the name of Jesus I put on and sink into the clothing of humility with the aspect having tasted Your Spirit realm of life. Lord, I pray that I can eat the unleavened bread of life and drink the wine from the vine of life. May You refresh me with the water of life that flows from the Father's throne and Your throne. May I have an abundant life where money does not matter but that I am rich in love, peace, and joy. May righteousness continue to flow in my veins as I am part of the last Adam's life. Amen.

Chapter 15: Clothed With Humility (Part 7)

AS WE GET MORE CONFIDENT in operating with the senses the Holy Spirit has given it is important that pride does not creep in. For this has been a major block to all the past revivals and one of the reasons why God's Kingdom does not advance the way it should. We are seeing the Great Harvest come in, but the Harvest workers must be shown the errors of past deceptions that have thwarted God's plan for the marching forward of His kingdom.

Danger of Pride Due to Awakened Senses

Jesus through the power of the Holy Spirit operated with all His senses but was able to resist pride. Because He is fully perfect in all ways, yet humble enough to love us when we go astray and help us come back. There is a warning given that we must adhere to.

In the *Final Quest Trilogy*, Rick Joyner describes the primary grace that Jesus gives us about the unknown present deception in our lives:

> The first grace that will keep you on the path of life is to know the level of your present deception. Deception involves anything that you do not understand as I do. Knowing the level of your present deception brings humility, and I give My grace to the humble.[54]

Jesus reveals to us that His grace is sufficient (see 2 Cor. 12:9a). We are to "be submissive to one another, and be clothed with humility, for God resists the proud, but gives grace to the humble" (1 Pet. 5:5b

NKJV). When you understand each deception in your life as Jesus does this is where it is written that through Jesus's knowledge of the enemies plans in your life are the given secret treasures of darkness and the hidden riches that are stored there (see Isaiah 45:3).

HUMILITY COVERS THE ARMOR

Rick Joyner also describes that our armor contains the glory that surrounds Him and what happens when you take it off as Wisdom/Jesus speaks in *The Final Quest Trilogy*:

> He then gestured toward me, so I looked at myself, pulling back the cloak of humility. I was stunned by what I saw. My armor contained the same glory that surrounded Him. I quickly covered it again with my cloak.[55]

> Every time you take off humility you will be blinded to the true light, and it will take time for you to be able to see it again.[56]

DO NOT TAKE YOUR EYES OFF JESUS

Why take the cloak off, you may ask? Because sometimes we get enamored in the glory realms of the Spirit, we forget that we are to stay humble. Curiosity gets the best because humility is a quality that must be put on and is part of the character of the new man (see Col. 3:12). The reason for being blinded is that "we can be mirrors that brightly reflect the glory of the Lord" (2 Cor. 3:18 TLB). We are thus warned to not look at the reflected glory of Jesus Christ by taking off the cloak of humility. This is when the beginning of pride comes in and you take your eyes off Jesus.

The true light is knowing that the battle is raging and that you took your eyes off the battlefield to look at yourself. We are instructed that we are to "seek Yahweh, all you humble of the land, who have kept his ordinances. Seek righteousness. Seek humility. It may be that you will be hidden in the day of Yahweh's anger" (Zep. 2:3).

WRAP YOURSELF IN HUMILITY

The warning of staying humble and not giving into to pride is that we are hidden in Christ Jesus, in God (see Col. 3:3) as Moses was hidden in the cleft of the rock so God's glorious face would not kill him (see Exo. 33:20-22). We are warned "to go into the caverns of the rocks, and into the clefts of the ragged rocks, from before the terror of Yahweh, and from the glory of his majesty, when he arises to shake the earth mightily" (Isa. 2:21).

Staying humble is seeking to stay humble. Making sure that humility is wrapped around us. Because as we reflect Jesus's glory to those around us, which is light, pure light, this cloak is put on so that we do not get blinded by the glory ourselves. As you stay humble, you are protected from the wrath of God when He declares World War III on this planet. To stay protected you must have a relationship with the Holy Spirit in which it shows that you are wearing humility *and* the fear of Yahweh which gives you wealth, honor, and life (see Pro. 22:4).

Walking in Humility's Clothing

Rick Joyner also describes the last day army of God by two things in which they are destined to reign in the empty seats as Jesus speaks in *The Final Quest Trilogy*:

> The Lord then looked at the galleries and said, "Those empty seats could have been filled in any generation. I gave the invitation to sit here to everyone who has called upon My name. They are still available. Now the last battle has come, and many who are last shall be first. These seats will be filled before the battle is over. Those who will sit here will be known by two things: **they will wear the mantle of humility, and they will have My likeness.**"[57]

As warriors of Christ Jesus we take our places together with the likeness of Jesus Christ who stand in this army united as One. We are a community of unity for "how good and pleasant it is when God's people live together in unity!" (Psa. 133:1 NIV). Another way of interpreting it is "How wonderful it is, how pleasant, when brothers live in harmony!" (Psa. 133:1 TLB). The analogy of unity and harmony is like when we praise the Lord Jesus in a fellowship and multiple voices in different octaves, timbers, and notes that are in different but making melody together. That is the harmony of unity of being a single new man. In Romans 12:5 (HCSB) it is written "in the same way we who are many are one body in Christ and individually members of one another."

FORMED IN TRIALS AND HUMILITY

The Holy Spirit declares through Isaiah writings that "the high and lofty One who inhabits eternity, whose name is Holy, says: 'I dwell in the high and holy place, with him also who is of a contrite and humble spirit, to revive the spirit of the humble, and to revive the heart of the contrite'" (Isa. 57:15). One of Jesus's heart's desires is to revive the contrite and humble spirit. That is true what a revival for those of the Way of Jesus.

To have a contrite heart is to be crushed or demolished to their ways and live like Jesus, whose desire was to participate in following our Father's direction and mission given. This crushing process is usually complete when all ego and pride are wiped away through trials and tribulations. Through this we surrender ourselves to God that He cleans up the ground where we stand by sweeping it until there is no more dust or remnants of sand specs of pride and ego left. They are left on the stone or slab. We then can be molded into the vessel He has designed when we were just a thought in His mind.

"For Yahweh takes pleasure in his people. He crowns the humble with salvation" (Psa. 149:4). Again, the beautifying process is the final touches of being formed and is adding the designs on the vessel. The touches can be designs which are Scriptures written on it declaring the name of Jesus and/or adding holy color to it as identification markers of the uniqueness of that vessel which bears the mark of approval.

THE LOVE BETWEEN THE FATHER AND SON

Jesus had perfect fellowship with the Father. There was no argument between them but perfect love for one another that is reflected in their relationship. It was a magnetic relationship because the Father lived in Jesus (see Joh. 14:10). Jesus was so obedient to His call that He died for it. But because of that death and submission the Father resurrected Jesus (see Gal. 1:1 NIV).

That is the type of relationship we need to have with the Holy Spirit. It is that type of devoted love that is deeper than any human bond can ever give. This is what true faithfulness between each other means. The magnitude of love that is displayed in humility is a devotion that that no grave of death can keep down.

THE UNDYING LOVE OF THE BRIDE

This love is undying and eternal that we have between God, Jesus, and the Holy Spirit. This love must first be reciprocated by the Bride and then the lost. Reaching out to the non-believers in God's love is a key component of the last-day revival/harvest. This type of love is only given because of Jesus's resurrection. I ask you to keep this love alive between each other that is faithful to each other. Do not let situations hold back agape love between each other that the spirit of death wants to bring to the Body and separate the Bride and the Bridegroom from each other.

"If therefore there is any exhortation in Christ, if any consolation of love, if any fellowship of the Spirit, if any tender mercies and compassion, make my joy full by being like-minded, having the same love, being of one accord, of one mind" (Phil. 2:1-2). There must be unity through humility that we must give each other through comforting each other in love. It is this love that is only given through relationship with the Holy Spirit that gives us the ability to provide affection and mercy.

This unity shows that we have the same purpose, and with this one mind comes unity because of the agreement on the strategy that the Holy Spirit has given the leadership for the task at hand. That task is the mission and purpose of that local church for fulfilling the calling of outreach to the lost and making disciples. When you make disciples, it is for the purpose the Apostle Paul wrote in Ephesians 4:12-16:

> for the perfecting of the saints, to the work of serving, to the building up of the body of Christ,until we all attain to the unity of the faith and of the knowledge of the Son of God, to a full grown man, to the measure of the stature of the fullness of Christ,that we may no longer be children, tossed back and forth and carried about with every wind of doctrine, by the trickery of men, in craftiness, after the wiles of error;but speaking truth in love, we may grow up in all things into him who is the head, Christ, from whom all the body, being fitted and knit together through that which every joint supplies, according to the working in measure of each individual part, makes the body increase to the building up of itself in love.

the Humbleness of the New Man

Paul writes to the church at Colosse, Timothy, Titus, and the church at Rome about the characteristics of how a Christian is to behave. I know from experience that when you mature through humbleness that it is easier to walk in the characteristics of the New Man. The verses written below are about those characteristics that are needed to describe humbleness and humility:

> ◇ Put on therefore, as God's chosen ones, holy and beloved, a heart of compassion, kindness, lowliness, humility, and

perseverance; bearing with one another, and forgiving each other, if any man has a complaint against any; even as Christ forgave you, so you also do. Above all these things, walk in love, which is the bond of perfection. And let the peace of God rule in your hearts, to which also you were called in one body, and be thankful (Col. 3:12-15).

- The Lord's servant must not quarrel, but be gentle toward all, able to teach, patient, in gentleness correcting those who oppose him: perhaps God may give them repentance leading to a full knowledge of the truth, and they may recover themselves out of the devil's snare, having been taken captive by him to his will (2 Tim. 2:24-26).

- Remind them to be in subjection to rulers and to authorities, to be obedient, to be ready for every good work,to speak evil of no one, not to be contentious, to be gentle, showing all humility toward all men (Tit. 3:1-2).

- Bless those who persecute you; bless, and don't curse.Rejoice with those who rejoice. Weep with those who weep. Be of the same mind one toward another. Don't set your mind on high things, but associate with the humble. Don't be wise in your own conceits (Rom. 12:14-16).

Work Ethics of the Humble Person

This passage in Ephesians is written down by Paul, it is inferred that we are to remain humble in our work ethic.

Servants, be obedient to those who according to the flesh are your masters, with fear and trembling, in singleness of your heart, as to Christ, not in the way of service only when eyes are on you, as men pleasers, but as servants of Christ, doing the will of God from the heart, with good will doing service as to the Lord, and not to men,knowing that whatever good thing each one does, he will receive the same good again from the Lord, whether he is bound or free. You masters, do the same things to them, and give up threatening, knowing that he who is both their Master and yours is in heaven, and there is no partiality with him (Eph. 6:5-9).

This is the relationship that a worker and boss should have. The bondservant/worker and the master/boss have a reciprocal relationship in the aspect that as Christians they serve the same Jesus Christ and are family. As workers, we work as if we are working for Christ which is what God the Father wants from the bottom of His heart. That is working in unity where we do our part for the common goal of the presented task.

I want to recap the following three things about this cloak/mantle of humility. First, it is plain to look at and not what you expect it to look like. Second, it is needed to see clearly in the Spirit realm where it was elaborated that all 5 senses are needed to understand the entire concept of the Body of Christ. Then third and lastly, it causes you to have discernment which is written below.

Humility Uses Discernment

As you have your senses sharpened by the Spirit with all understanding in humility the concept of full discernment is brought to the spiritually mature. You need to have wisdom to discern. In the book of Proverbs, it is written that like the son, the reading is to be taken personal:

...turn your ear to wisdom, and apply your heart to understanding; yes, if you call out for discernment, and lift up your voice for understanding; if you seek her as silver, and search for her as for hidden treasures: then you will understand the fear of Yahweh, and find the knowledge of God (Elohim) (Pro. 2:2-5).

In a previous section we discussed wisdom. As we listen to the wisdom of the Spirit written in His Holy Word, we are to cry out for discernment and in a voice whether it is audible or not we pray for the understanding that accompanies wisdom. Wisdom and discernment are precious treasures that are hidden that must be searched out. Like silver it must be refined in your life.

When searching for wisdom it is to be administered in a function that you understand only in God's Word. You are to chew on it, slowly digest it, accept it, then practice it. If you also see in this passage that when the knowledge of wisdom is gained through the understanding of the fear of the Lord or Yahweh. Then the practice of discernment is instituted in our lives which is then acknowledged that the knowledge of God is gained.

As you mature in the Lord you know that you go from milk/baby food into solid food. This graduation in the natural is reflected in the Spirit that "solid food is for those who are full grown, who by reason of use have their senses exercised to discern good and evil" (Heb. 5:14). The more mature you are in the Lord, the more you see things from God's point of view.

The maturity process is not based on age in the concept of time in the natural. What I mean by that is if you accept Jesus at the age of 55 you are spiritually immature as the person who accepted Jesus at the age of seven might be more mature when they are twenty-five because they may have studied and applied Scripture throughout their lives. It is the solid food that makes the person grow. You learn from the elders what to do and not to do. You then learn to apply it in your lives. It is reading the Scriptures and applying them to different aspects of your life.

"For the word of God is living and active, and sharper than any two-edged sword, piercing even to the dividing of soul and spirit, of both joints and marrow, and is able to discern the thoughts and intentions of the heart" (Heb. 4:12). When you have a knowledge of the Word of God that is living and active in you because the Holy Spirit resides in you, you administer it with love because of the humility. Solomon wrote that "whoever keeps the commandment shall not come to harm, and his wise heart will know the time and procedure.For there is a time and procedure for every purpose" (Ecc. 8:5-6b).

Are you praying for wisdom every day? Do you need to ask for wisdom in all situations? We are to rely on Abba for everything. Especially when talking to people. We are to be sensitive to how they perceive the witness of the Spirit. The witness of the Spirit walks with discernment.

In Ezekiel, the prophet was describing the ministry and the regulations of the priests of God in his time when the Levitical priesthood was still active where he wrote that "they shall teach My people *the difference* between the holy and the unholy, and cause them to discern between the unclean and the clean" (Eze. 44:23 NKJV). We see that discernment was necessary in the Levitical priesthood, and so much more in the Melchizedek priesthood. This New Covenant priesthood is unchanging or unwavering.

Jesus the High Priest tells us priests that we should know the difference between the holy and unholy ways in our life. It is not just a materialistic realm of idols made of natural substances or the worship of nature, but it is knowing that the pursuit of holiness in our lives is acceptable. When we pursue holiness, that which is unholy becomes disdainful. You see God's goodness and then you become more of His reflection as you pursue holiness.

By this knowledge of the holy we can use wisdom and discernment in our lives to judge things by authority given to us as kings, not tyrants over that which has been entrusted to us. Whether it is as a parent, person in authority, or our work in life, we must do it by holiness. It is through His love that we fully develop humility.

As you learn to discern, do not do it on your own, learn from seasoned Christians. There are many mistakes that can be made. But as you mature in wisdom and humility, you will be able to know what is from the Holy Spirit and what is not. This is done with the knowledge of the fear of the Lord or Yahweh.

a book of Memory

In Malachi the Lord provides comfort to us that there is *a book of memory* for those that fear Him and meditate on His name. The revealed name of Jesus is the highest name where the whole family in heaven and on earth is named after (see Eph. 3:14b-15). Below is the Scripture that reveals the Book of Remembrance found in Malachi 3:16-18.

> Then those who feared Yahweh spoke one with another; and Yahweh listened, and heard, and a <u>book of memory</u> was written before him, for those who feared Yahweh, and who honored his name. They shall be mine," says Yahweh of Armies, "my own possession in the day that I make, and I will spare them, as a man spares his own son who serves him. Then you shall return and discern between the righteous and the wicked, between him who serves God and him who doesn't serve him (Mal. 3:16-18 underline mine).

The promise given is that the God of Heavenly Armies says that the nation of Israel is His as well as the blood bought Church. Looking at it from the point of view that the Church and national Israel are one tree and a treasure that God desires that through "humility and the fear of Yahweh is wealth, honor, and life" (Pro. 22:4). Those riches are compared to full unity of national Israel being grafted back into the Olive Tree that they are. They are the root of the Church. With that comes the honor and life restoration of the Spirit where they will be One with Christ Jesus.

This is a future prophecy that also declares that all of Israel and Judah will be given discernment to judge between the righteous and the wicked, and those that serve God or serve any form of the kingdom darkness. This will happen with the help of the Messiah and the whole Body of Christ activated and mature as a spotless and wrinkle free Bride.

Prophet Zephaniah encourages us in chapter 2 verse 13 that we are to "seek Yahweh, all you humble of the land, who have kept his ordinances. Seek righteousness. Seek humility. It may be that you will be hidden in the day of Yahweh's anger" (Zep. 2:3).

As we mature in humility, we are to seek it like we seek His righteousness in our lives and that we are to seek Father Yahweh. Are you actively searching for Him to be able to administer love to a lost world of sinners? Are you able to have compassion for those that need compassion? Can you serve those that spit and despise/revile you? It is difficult and must be done without bitterness in the heart. That bitterness can only be taken away by forgiving those that hurt, sin, or trespass against you. But through much grace, tender mercies, and seeking humility, will we be able to retain love for the unlovable. Remember to seek Abba!

To Seek the Lord YAHWEH

As we march forward as a united love seeking and caring family of Christians we will not bow to other idols in the land. The Israelites had started to worship false gods because they could not wait for Moses to receive the instructions from the Lord or Yahweh (see Exodus 32). As we stay humble, before the King of Glory, remember we must not set our eyes on the things of the world for happiness. Our delight must be in Jesus Christ!

We are to seek the Lord or Yahweh our God, and we will find *Him* if we seek Him with all our heart and with all our hearts and souls (see Deu. 4:29 AMP). David instructed that we are to "give thanks to Yahweh. Call on his name. Make what he has done known among the peoples. Sing to him. Sing praises to him. Tell of all his marvelous works. Glory in his holy name. Let the heart of those who seek Yahweh rejoice" (1 Chr. 16:8-10). How amazing is this that as we are commissioned to seek Him that we are to engage in the act of singing to Him. We sing to Him also through the revealed name of Jesus.

I want to let you know that the lovesick heart of the humble will be granted favor because of what He has done and what Jesus will do. Try singing the psalms to Him. As you pray to Him out loud, rejoice because Jesus tells us what He has done, what He does, and what He will do.

Jesus spoke to us with the message that "whoever therefore humbles himself as this little child is the greatest in the Kingdom of Heaven" (Mat. 18:4). We are to be like little children in the aspect of searching for Him through humbleness. The humbling process starts with "the just" seeking Him daily.

We are instructed by the prophet Isaiah that we are to "seek Yahweh while he may be found. Call on him while he is near" (Isa. 55:6). Why must we seek Him while He may be found? Because to those that do not seek after Him, He cannot be found but to those that seek, He will be found because He really is not far away (see Act. 17:27).

The Lord Jesus wants to remind us that "for everyone who exalts himself will be humbled, and whoever humbles himself will be exalted" (Luk. 14:11). As we seek Him, we must not be arrogant that we can find Him. Sometimes He likes to mysteriously hide Himself by playing a game of "hide and seek" so that when He is found you may "live" (see Amo.5:4b).

The Humble Receives Justice

Jesus, who is the wisdom speaking through Solomon instructs us that we are to "seek Yahweh, all you humble of the land, who have kept his ordinances. Seek righteousness. Seek humility" (Zep. 2:3). Yet God "surely he mocks the mockers, but he gives grace to the humble" (Pro.

3:34). This phrase shows that as we continue to seek God's holiness, love, tender mercies, etc. that he protects us from those that come against us. Staying humble is one of the keys of the kingdom that Jesus has given His Bride. As we continue to embrace His humility, we are encouraged by the process of humbling ourselves under the mighty hand of God, that He may exalt us in due time, casting all our worries upon Him, for He cares for us (see 1 Pet. 5:6-7).

We are in a time as part of the Last Generation "ZION"/Zion Army that certain parts of the Body are commissioned with the helping of the restoration of David's Tabernacle of Praise and Worship. As they are being restored to the fullness and usage in His Kingdom it written that this is done for this purpose "that the rest of men may seek after the Lord; all the Gentiles who are called by my name, says the Lord, who does all these things" (Act. 15:17).

The things in reference are rebuilding the walls of the tabernacle of David. It requires a body of blood washed saints that do not discriminate between racial colors or genders. They uphold God's morality in a sinful world that brings about His love for holy conviction which leads to repentance.

It is "evil men [who] don't understand justice; but those who seek Yahweh understand it fully" (Pro. 28:5 brackets mine). For "Yahweh is good to those who wait for him, to the soul who seeks him" (Lam. 3:25). It is "Yahweh [who] upholds the humble. He brings the wicked down to the ground" (Psa. 147:6 brackets mine). "For you will save the afflicted people, but the arrogant eyes you will bring down" (Psa. 18:27). "He will guide the humble in justice. He will teach the humble his way" (Psa. 25:9).

There is a theme that is woven above that the Lord or Yahweh is good to those that wait and seek Him. It is to those that He protects and gives justice righteously because of the person's heart of not being prideful but staying continually humble before Him that they understand everything that pertains to God's justice spiritually, morally, ethically, judicially.

GOD PROTECTS AND AVENGES THE HUMBLE

Because when He protects us against the wicked that gives us evil, disdainful looks through wicked eyes of condemnation or those seeking to kill us or have killed those in the past. "For he who avenges blood remembers them. He doesn't forget the cry of the afflicted" (Psa. 9:12). It is His word that says "Arise, O Lord! O God, lift up Your hand; forget not the humble [patient and crushed]" (Psa. 10:12 AMPC). It is through His hand that justice is administered. We ask that that by His very power that He does not forget the humble petitioner.

I want to encourage you that it is God who takes vengeance, not us. Paul writes "Don't seek revenge yourselves, beloved, but give place to God's wrath. For it is written, '**Vengeance belongs to me; I will repay, says the Lord**'" (Rom. 12:19 bold mine).

THE FATHER'S INSTRUCTIONS

Every spiritual battle is done in "My Son's name. The name of Jesus."

BEING CLOTHED WITH HUMILITY PART 7

Holy Spirit in the name of Jesus I put on and sink into the clothing of humility for seeking Yahweh. I ask that as I grow closer to You Abba Father that my love towards You becomes more and more real. Let it become an undying love. Let my heart not grow cold. With this eternal love let me grow in discerning in the Spirit realm with an increase of the Holy Spirit in my life. I request that as I grow in the prophetic realm of discerning that I am able to bring or manifest this into witnessing more for You. Let me proclaim the Kingdom of God with such boldness that I am a walking flame of fire. Let my light shine and say that they will know that I have been with You, my Lord Jesus. Lord, I want to thank You for clothing me in true humility that defeats false pride. I am thankful that You keep a book of memory/remembrance. I also thank

You that You protect me and avenge for me against my enemies. Let me walk in Your love by not taking revenge or vengeance but instill in my heart a peace and confidence that You will repay and take vengeance on my behalf. Amen.

PART III – THE PRIESTLY HEADDRESS

Chapter 16: The Turban of Justice with The Crown of Holiness

THE TURBAN OF JUSTICE

Like the Robe of Justice there is a turban of Justice. As previously discussed about the justice of God through Christ, our redeemer, let us look at this through the eyes of the Spirit. For it is written that "my justice was like a robe and a turban *or* a diadem *or* a crown" (Job 29:14b AMPC). Since Job is considered the oldest book in the Bible, it can safely be said that the turban has been used since the earliest days of humanity.

In the beginning, it is written that the wardrobe of Joshua the High Priest and the dirty clothes that he wore needed to purged and new garments put on; the final garment to put on is the turban. In Zechariah 3:4 it says that the Angel of the Lord or Yahweh is clothing Joshua. It is written about Zechariah stating the declaring "then I said, 'Let them put a clean turban on his head.' So, a clean turban was placed on his head, and they clothed him in garments..." (Zec. 3:5).

The turban represents that we should have upon our head pure motives. Our motives should be with clean hearts and minds which include devoting the thought patterns after the things of the Lord Jesus and the Holy Spirit. Edifying oneself to be so heavenly minded that you are Earthly good.

The making of the turban is commanded that "Make the turban out of fine linen...for Aaron's sons... you should also make...turbans to mark their honor and dignity" (Exo. 28:39-40 Common English Bible (CEB)). Just to reiterate that the fine line is the righteous acts of the saints (see Rev. 19:8). The second part that was added to the turban was a Crown of Holiness or "Holy Crown" (see Lev. 8:9).

The Crown of Holiness

Below are the descriptions of the holy crown. The first usage of the holy crown are the instructions given by the Father, "You shall also make a plate of pure gold and engrave on it, *like* the engraving of a signet: HOLINESS TO THE LORD " (Exo. 28:36 NKJV). In the World English Bible, it is written "You shall make a plate of pure gold, and engrave on it, like the engravings of a signet, 'HOLY TO YAHWEH.'" (Exo. 28:36)

The second usage of the holy crown is when the Israelites completed it. "They made the plate of the holy crown of pure gold, and wrote on it an inscription, like the engravings of a signet: "HOLY TO YAHWEH". They tied to it a lace of blue, to fasten it on the turban above, as Yahweh commanded Moses" (Exo. 39:30-31).

The crown is made of gold. As gold has been written about in detail in *The Melchizedek Priesthood Garments* by the author: gold is the purity and the Divine nature of God living in us. We are to wear this Divine nature in the concept that we will one day be like Him, eternal, completely filled with the wisdom of the Spirit, and not prideful. With the Divine nature living in us we have an engraving of the Father saying that we are holy to Him. This is part of the new birth that we are holy from the moment we are Spiritually born as a Christian, yet we still must practice holiness.

A lifestyle of holiness

It is written by Apostle Peter that "just as he who called you is holy, you yourselves also be holy in all of your behavior; because it is written, 'You shall be holy; for I am holy'" (1 Pet. 1:15-16). Whatever we do, we must remember that we are part of a holy priesthood (see 1 Pet. 2:5). We are part of a priesthood that is forever and unchanging (see Heb. 7:24). We are instructed that we are to "pursue the goal of peace along with everyone—and holiness as well, because no one will see the Lord without it" (Heb. 12:14 CEB).

Holiness is something that we should always pursue. In the previous written chapters on being *clothed with humility* and seeing the Lord during this time, it is about knowing Him through the five senses. To see the Lord is also a reference to His return and/or being in heaven with Him. Holiness should be done out of love and not just law. It is out of God's love that we are allowed to be intimate with Him in holiness.

When the glory cloud comes forth it is with the holiness of God. This is a time when you see yourself and who you are before Him. This is the holiness that men must see us as. We are to imitate the Lord Jesus Christ (see 1 Cor. 11:1).

JESUS, THE TRUE NEW MAN

Jesus is called "the Holy One of God" (Mar. 1:24). As we imitate Christ, and to fulfill the Mosaic law in the aspect of holiness Jesus had to be holy. We are instructed that we are to let our human bodies be servants *of* righteousness. For holiness is a fruit that we produce because we are now servants of God which produces everlasting life (see Rom. 6:19).

As we reflect the holiness of Jesus Christ, we know that Jesus is glorious in holiness. At the transfiguration of Jesus on the Mount we notice that "His face shone like the sun, and his garments became as white as the light" (Mat. 17:2). It is that holiness that we get to gaze upon God the Father. He is described as glorious in holiness (see Exo.15:11). We are the image of Christ Jesus through putting on the new man which is created in true holiness (see Eph. 4:24).

It is that new man that we put on that we are also given the right to be holy without being holy by the Law of Moses. "The law has become our tutor to bring us to Christ, that we might be justified by faith" (Gal. 3:24).

As we can now worship the God of Holiness and have that as part of our lives, we can follow the instructions to "Worship the Lord in the beauty *and* majesty of His holiness [as the creator and source of holiness]" (Psa. 29:2b AMP). As we worship the Lord Jesus, and if we have sin in our lives, we are also to get cleansed of it as we confess our sins to Him. The Holy Spirit provides us with the cleansing agent of the blood of Jesus to make us holy once again and keep going on in life.

CHOOSING TO STAY HOLY

We choose to stay holy because it is something to pursue while we work out our salvation with fear and trembling (see Phil. 2:12). As we continue to work through our salvation, we should continue to bear the light that Jesus Christ has given us. That light is the Word, Himself, Jesus Christ. Can you fearfully say that you stand in holiness and that your light is shining brightly? If it is, praise the Lord! I will also ask, if your light is not shining as bright as it once did, repent, ask God to cleanse you, worship and seek Jesus so that you may reflect His light in your life.

CO-MINGLING OF HOLINESS AND JUSTICE

As your light shines in holiness with the Holy Spirit seeing through you the blue cord that is tied and fastened between the turban and the holy crown takes place after the garments and robes of the *Šô'ēriym* (Gatekeepers) are put on (see Exo. 29:6, 39:31). The blue cord that links the turban and the holy crown represents the grace of God in a Believer's life. It is the grace that allows holiness and justice to co-mingle together.

This co-mingling is because as justice is administered the administrator of justice is holy. As a *Šô'ēriym* the justice that is provided is to rightly apply the Word of God in our lives and love into another's life. It is exhorting, encouraging, rebuking them with unconditional Divine love that shows and reflects Jesus Christ. To be able to have any level of discernment you must have the Mind of Christ or the Mind of the Spirit.

The Mind of Christ (Mind of the Spirit)

Paul instructs the Corinthians that "the natural man doesn't receive the things of God's Spirit, for they are foolishness to him, and he can't know them, because they are spiritually discerned. But he who is spiritual discerns all things, and he himself is judged by no one. 'For who has known the mind of the Lord, that he should instruct him?' But we have Christ's mind" (1 Cor. 2:14-16).

Paul also instructs the Romans, that "so too the [Holy] Spirit comes to our aid *and* bears us up in our weakness; for we do not know what prayer to offer *nor* how to offer it worthily as we ought, but the Spirit Himself goes to meet our supplication *and* pleads in our behalf with unspeakable yearnings *and* groanings too deep for utterance. And He Who searches the hearts of men knows what is in the mind of the [Holy] Spirit [what His intent is], because the Spirit intercedes *and* pleads [before God] in behalf of the saints according to *and* in harmony with God's will" (Rom. 8:26-27 AMPC).

There are two differences between the mind of Christ and the mind of the Spirit. They work with each other. The Christian uses the mind of Christ to judge and discern all thing because He already judged that person as righteous because of the integrity of his heart as being holy.

With the mind of the Spirit, the Holy Spirit working through us makes intercession to Jesus on behalf with the person praying in their human language, spiritual language (which is received with the Baptism of the Holy Spirit), and/or groanings that have no words to them.

To use them in unity, it is usually the prophetic person or prophet/prophetess that received the revelation on how to pray for that person and help them intercede for them. That intercession can be used to help them get over a spiritual funk by encouragement in their life and restoring them to get them in a right position with God the Father.

How to Access the Mind of Christ

As I started to ponder this, the Holy Spirit kept showing me the number 72. It represents the 72 hours that Jesus was in the grave (see Mat. 12:40; Act. 10:40). As we were raised up from the grave with Jesus, we then have the right to seek God's face (see 1 Chr. 16:11; Psa. 105:4). We know that the mind of Christ is really another expression of the mind of the Messiah or the Anointed One.

Where is the mind located? It is logically in the head, and as Jesus is the head of the Body of Christ, it is our duty to seek Him. As we seek His face, we really seek the face of Jesus. For Jesus said, "He who has seen me has seen the Father" (Joh. 14:9). To seek Jesus's face is to seek the expression of God's features of love, righteousness, peace, and joy.

Part of the mind of Christ is to know Jesus as intimately as anyone else. We should be able to discern His thoughts because we know His Word or love letters/scrolls to us. His ways become our ways, and His thoughts become our thoughts. I will reiterate, spending time in communion with the Holy Spirit allows us to know the mind of the Spirit. Remember, it is a dialogue, not a monologue, so listening with our spiritual ears is necessary.

As we glory in the presence of God and learn to commune with understanding His ways become our ways. We then can be transformed into the image of Christ Jesus going from glory to glory. This transformation is only given by renewing our mind with the Scriptures, and communion of the Spirit (see Rom. 12:2; 2 Cor. 3:18).

It is the Holy Spirit, who is our seal, promise, and guarantee that allows us to commune with God. The seal of the Spirit location is in our foreheads. In my personal experiences that is when the Spirit of God is moving on a person, the face starts to shine. They start to glow per se then the Spirit moves deeper in them and through them. It is written that "They [His servants/children] will see his face, and his name will be on their foreheads" (Rev. 22:4 brackets mine).

E. Swedenborg wrote the following about the forehead:

The forehead with man corresponds to his love, therefore they who are in celestial love (that is, in love to the Lord from the Lord) are said to have a mark on their foreheads, by which is signified that they are under the Lord's protection, because they are in His love.[58]

The Mind of Christ Reveals the Father's Heart

As Father God wants His family to know His mind, we should also know His heart. The heart of God is really love. It is out of His love that He sent Jesus (see Joh. 3:16). God wants to show up and most of the time is rejected out of fear.

Michal Ann Goll testified in her husband, Jim W. Goll's book *The Lost Art of Intercession* the stance of the corporate body reaction generally with God's manifest Presence and how He feels about it:

We as a corporate body of believers often recoil when He really answers our sung prayers and touches us with His glory and fire! We back up and say, 'No! You're coming too close.' Meanwhile, God is saying, 'Do you realize that all of those songs you've been singing to Me are arousing My love?

I am coming to you and you don't even know that it's Me.'[59]

Why are we afraid of His coming? Is it because we do not want to change and go from glory to glory? Generally, the Holy Spirit is frightening because He stirs our raw emotions. His holiness is really something that is not bearable to human flesh. His presence exposes everything about us to Him. It will also show us what is in the deep recesses of our heart which allows us to confess it towards Him. It is out of His love He wants to show you your heart by showing up.

Are you willing to search the deep things of God which lead to knowing Him and His face? Do you really love Him enough to do this? I challenge you as you keep pursuing Him, that you do not let your fleshly fear overcome you and lose out on His blessings of rich supernatural encounters that renew your mind, spirit, soul, and body daily. Do you dare to put on the turban of justice with the holy crown? If so, let us make it a daily way of life that His ways are our ways.

PUTTING ON THE TURBAN OF JUSTICE AND CROWN OF HOLINESS

Holy Spirit in the name of Jesus I put on the holy turban of justice with the crown of holiness. I ask that as You teach me more of Your ways that I can seek justice and mercy which are the foundations of Your throne. Let me gaze upon Your face Jesus as I am being conformed more to Your image daily. Let me deny myself and crucify my flesh so that I can live in our Father's presence daily. Make me a reflection of Your love Abba Father. Let my heart express Your love to everyone daily. Help me to control my emotions so that I am known as being with my elder brother Jesus. Let my face shine with Your light that my lamp is overflowing with the oil of the Holy Spirit and that I can let this light shine in the darkest of places. Amen.

EPILOGUE

CLOTHED WITH THE MELCHIZEDEKIAN Priesthood
Garments and Robes

In Zechariah 3:4b-5 (CEB) the Father and the Angel of Lord declare to Joshua the follow, "'Look, I have removed your guilt from you. Put on priestly robes' He said, 'Put a clean turban upon his head.' So they put the clean turban upon his head, and they dressed him in garments.'" As this reference has a two-fold meaning. The Angel of Lord is a reference to the Pre-Incarnate Jesus Christ.

The symbolism is that it was the Father and Jesus dressing Joshua the High Priest from dirty, sinful, unholy garments and reclothed him with clean, purified, holy garments. For it is written that "He [the High Priest or priests] shall put on the holy linen tunic. He shall have the linen trousers on his body, and shall put on the linen sash, and he shall be clothed with the linen turban. They are the holy garments. " (Lev. 16:4 brackets mine).

The other meaning is that as Jesus, who is Joshua our High Priest in the Melchizedekian priesthood (see Heb. 6:20). Jesus put on our dirty, sinful priestly robes, washed them in His blood, and made us a "holy royal priesthood" (see 1 Pet. 2:5, 9). Once we became part of His "holy royal priesthood" we can then be clothed with holy garments.

Now that the knowledge of the garments as *Šô'ēriym* (Gatekeepers), I ask you that you allow the Holy Spirit to dress you with the twenty-four (24) priestly garments in the following sequential order from the wardrobe:

1. The Garment of Light or Joseph's Colorful Tunic.

2. The Garment of Salvation.

3. Clothed in Scarlet.

4. The Garment of Salvation/<u>Deliverance</u>.

5. The Garment of Praise.

6. Clothed with Gladness.

7. Clothed with Righteousness.

8. Clothed with Pure Bright Linen and White Robes and Palm Branches in Hands.

9. Raiment of Needlework.

10. Clothing of Gold.

11. Clothed and Girded with Strength

12. Clothed with a Cloud.

13. Clothed with Our Heavenly Habitation.

14. Apparel of Red.

15. The Garments of Vengeance.

16. Chests Wrapped with Golden Sashes.

17. Clothed with Purple.

18. Clothed with "Hode" and "Haw-dawr'" or Splendor and Majesty/Honor.

19. The Fine Linen Ephod Robe.

20. Robe of Righteousness.

21. Robe of Justice.

22. Clothed with Humility.

23. Turban of Justice

24. The Crown of Holiness.

The Promises of the Priesthood

In Zechariah 3:6-8b are the promises of God to Jesus and His priests.

Yahweh's angel protested to Joshua, saying,"Yahweh of Armies says:

'If you will walk in my ways, and if you will follow my instructions, then you also shall judge my house, and shall also keep my courts, and I will give you a place of access among these who stand by. Hear now, Joshua the high priest, you and your fellows who sit before you; for they are men who are a sign: for, behold, I will bring out my servant, the Branch.

The promises given to Joshua/Jesus Christ the High Priest will be able to able to administrate the following according to verse 7:

1. Judge His Father's house.

1. Have charge of the courts of Heaven.

1. Provided places to walk among those that stand in the courts of Heaven.

As the companions of Joshua/Jesus the High Priest we are promised the following according to verses 8a-b. Jesus said "I am the vine. You are the branches" (Joh. 15:5). As the branches from the Branch or vine like Jesus our High Priest we can sit before Him rendering verdicts according to the order of Melchizedek. This is a wondrous sign given to us as our heritage according to Isaiah 54:17 which states "'No weapon that is formed against you will prevail; and you will condemn every tongue that rises against you in judgment. This is the heritage of Yahweh's servants, and their righteousness is of me,' says Yahweh." "Arise! Let's go up to Zion to Yahweh our God" (Jer. 31:6). For the Melchizedekian priesthood is comprised of redeemed Jews and Gentiles. Praise Yah or Hallelujah! Praise our One and Only Redeemer Jesus Chris the High Priest of the Order of Melchizedek.

ENDNOTES

1   blueletterbible.org, meh-eel, https://www.blueletterbible.org/lexicon/h4598/kjv/wlc/0-1/.

2   Derek Prince, *Spiritual Warfare Kindle Edition - Headquarters-The Heavenlies; The Battlefield-Our Minds!:*, (New Kensington, Pennsylvania: Whitaker House, 1987), Locations 616-622.

3   blueletterbible.org, naw-shak', https://www.blueletterbible.org/lexicon/h5401/kjv/wlc/0-1.

4   blueletterbible.org, naw-sak', https://www.blueletterbible.org/lexicon/h5400/kjv/wlc/0-1.

5   thefreedictionary.com, homage, https://www.thefreedictionary.com/Hommage. American Heritage® Dictionary of the English language, Fifth Edition. Copyright © 2016 by Houghton Mifflin Harcourt Publishing Company. Published by Houghton Mifflin Harcourt Publishing Company. All rights reserved.

6   Derek Prince, *Spiritual Warfare Kindle Edition - Headquarters-The Heavenlies; The Battlefield-Our Minds!:*, (New Kensington, Pennsylvania: Whitaker House, 1987), Location 311.

7   Ibid., Location 313.

8   blueletterbible.org, *aw-done'*, https://www.blueletterbible.org/lexicon/h113/kjv/wlc/0-1.

9   blueletterbible.org, *or-maw'*, https://www.blueletterbible.org/lexicon/h6195/kjv/wlc/0-1.

10   Derek Prince, *Spiritual Warfare Kindle Edition - Headquarters-The Heavenlies; The Battlefield-Our Minds!:*, (New Kensington, Pennsylvania: Whitaker House, 1987), Location 434.

11   Melissa Turmino, *THE ULTIMATE GUIDE TO THE COLORS IN THE BIBLE*, (Thinkaboutsuchthings.com 2020), pp. 38-39.

12   youtube.com, Pure Life Ministries, *The Fear of the Lord is the Beginning of Wisdom | 20 Truths that Help the Battle with Porn Addiction*,   https://www.youtube.com/watch?v=6BwGOrFKSVw, 2019.

13   Ibid.

14   Derek Prince, *Spiritual Warfare Kindle Edition - Headquarters-The Heavenlies; The Battlefield-Our Minds!:*, (New Kensington, Pennsylvania: Whitaker House, 1987), Locations 821-827.

15   nhs.uk, *How to get Vitamin D from sunlight Healthy body*, Crown copyright,   https://www.nhs.uk/live-well/healthy-body/how-to-get-vitamin-d-from-sunlight.

16   biblestudy.org, *The Meaning of Numbers: The Number 66, https://www.biblestudy.org/bibleref/meaning-of-numbers-in-bible/ 66.html.*

17   Derek Prince, *Spiritual Warfare Kindle Edition – Headquarters-The Heavenlies; The Battlefield-Our Minds!:*, (New Kensington, Pennsylvania: Whitaker House, 1987), Locations 874-880.

18   Derek Prince, *Spiritual Warfare Kindle Edition - Headquarters-The Heavenlies; The Battlefield-Our Minds!:*, (New Kensington, Pennsylvania: Whitaker House, 1987), Locations 313-332.

19   Derek Prince, *Spiritual Warfare Kindle Edition - Headquarters-The Heavenlies; The Battlefield-Our Minds!:*, (New Kensington, Pennsylvania: Whitaker House, 1987), Locations 810-817.

20 Martin Luther, and Fredrick H. Hedge, *A Mighty Fortress is Our God,* https://hymnary.org/text/a_mighty_fortress_is_our_god_a_bulwark, public domain.

21 Mike Bickle, Library International House of Prayer University, *STUDIES THE BEUATY OF GOD: Session 6* Behold a Throne and One Who Sits on It (Rev. 4:2) notes on 21 April 2006, pg. 3.

22 Ibid., pg. 2.

23 Ibid., pg. 5.

24 Ibid., pg. 6.

25 Rick Joyner, *The Final Quest Trilogy – The Final Quest*, (Morning Star Fellowship, sold by Barnes & Noble, 2018), pp. 41-42.

26 David Guzik, *PSALM 149 – THE HIGH PRAISES OF GOD AND A TWO-EDGED SWORD*, The Enduring Word Bible Commentary, 2020, https://enduringword.com/bible-commentary/psalm-149

27 blueletterbible.org, *mas-saw'*, https://www.blueletterbible.org/lexicon/ h4853/kjv/wlc/0-11.

28 Rick Joyner, *The Final Quest Trilogy – The Final Quest*, (Morning Star Fellowship, sold by Barnes & Noble, 2018), pg. 42.

29 gotquestions.org, *What does it mean that Zerubbabel was the LORD's signet ring (Haggai 2:23)?*, https://www.gotquestions.org/Zerubbabel-signet-ring.html. January 4, 2022.

30 Rick Joyner, *The Final Quest Trilogy – The Final Quest*, (Morning Star Fellowship, sold by Barnes & Noble, 2018), pg. 102.

31 Ibid., pg. 82.

[32] Ibid., pg. 41.

[33] James W. Goll, *The Seer*, (Shippensburg, Pennsylvania: Destiny Image Publishers, Inc., 2004), pp. 34-43.

[34] Ibid., p. 54.

[35] Ibid., pp. 57-59.

[36] Ibid., pp. 59-60.

[37] Ibid., pp. 60-62.

[38] Ibid., pg. 62.

[39] Ibid., pg. 62.

[40] Ibid., pg. 62.

[41] blueletterbible.org, hor'-as-is, https://www.blueletterbible.org/lexicon/g3706/kjv/lxx/0-1.

[42] blueletterbible.org, kwaw-mad', https://www.blueletterbible.org/lexicon/h2530/kjv/wlc/0-1.

[43] Jane Hamon, *DISCERNMENT: the Essential Guide to HEARING the VOICE OF GOD*, (Bloomington, Minnesota: Chosen Books, 2019), pp. 22-23.

[44] Ibid., pg. 27.

[45] Jim W. Goll, *The Seer*, (Shippensburg, Pennsylvania: Destiny Image Publishers, Inc., 2004), pg. 63.

[46] Ibid., pp. 64-65.

[47] Ibid., pp. 65-66.

[48] Ibid., pg. 67.

[49] Ibid., pg. 67.

[50] James W. Goll, *The Coming Prophetic Revolution* (Grand Rapids, Michigan: Chosen Books, 2001), p. 125.

51 James W. Goll, *The Beginner's Guide to Hearing God* [E-pub] (Ventura, California: Regal From Gospel Light, 2008), 61-63%.

52 Biblical Hermeneutics, *Unfamiliar metaphors in Hosea 14:6-7*, https://hermeneutics.stackexchange.com/questions/1894/unfamiliar-metaphors-in-hosea-146-7, 2012.

53 Jim W. Goll, *The Lost Art of Intercession: Restoring the Power and Passion of the Watch of the Lord*, (Shippensburg, Pennsylvania: Revival Press an imprint of Destiny Image® Publishers, Inc., 1997), pp. 38-39.

54 Rick Joyner, *The Final Quest Trilogy – The Final Quest*, (Morning Star Fellowship, sold by Barnes & Noble, 2018), pg. 91.

55 Rick Joyner, *The Final Quest Trilogy – The Final Quest*, (Morning Star Fellowship, sold by Barnes & Noble, 2018), pg. 102.

56 Rick Joyner, *The Final Quest Trilogy – The Call*, (Morning Star Fellowship, sold by Barnes & Noble, 2018), pg. 211.

57 Rick Joyner, *The Final Quest Trilogy – The Call*, (Morning Star Fellowship, sold by Barnes & Noble, 2018), pg. 84.

58 E. Swedenborg, *Spiritual Meaning of Forehead*, http://www.biblemeanings.info/Words/Body/Forehead.htm, 2002.

59 Jim W. Goll, *The Lost Art of Intercession: Restoring the Power and Passion of the Watch of the Lord*, (Shippensberg, Pennsylvania: Revival Press an imprint of Destiny Image® Publishers, Inc., 1997), pg. 112.

BIBLIOGRAPHY

BOOKS

James W. Goll, *The Beginner's Guide to Hearing God* [E-pub] (Ventura, California: Regal From Gospel Light, 2008)

James W. Goll, *The Coming Prophetic Revolution* (Grand Rapids, Michigan: Chosen Books, 2001)

Jim W. Goll, *The Lost Art of Intercession: Restoring the Power and Passion of the Watch of the Lord*, (Shippensburg, Pennsylvania: Revival Press an imprint of Destiny Image® Publishers, Inc., 1997)

Jim W. Goll, *The Seer: The Prophetic Power of Visions, Dreams, and Open Heavens*, (Shippensburg, Pennsylvania: Destiny Image® Publishers, Inc., 2004)

Jane Hamon, *DISCERNMENT: the Essential Guide to HEARING the VOICE OF GOD*, (Bloomington, Minnesota: Chosen Books, 2019)

Rick Joyner, *The Final Quest Trilogy – The Call*, (Morning Star Fellowship, sold by Barnes & Noble, 2018)

Rick Joyner, *The Final Quest Trilogy – The Final Quest*, (Morning Star Fellowship, sold by Barnes & Noble, 2018)

Derek Prince, *Spiritual Warfare Kindle Edition - Headquarters-The Heavenlies; The Battlefield-Our Minds!:*, (New Kensington, Pennsylvania: Whitaker House, 1987)

Melissa Turmino, *THE ULTIMATE GUIDE TO THE COLORS IN THE BIBLE*, (Thinkaboutsuchthings.com 2020)

Articles/Study Notes/Websites

Biblical Hermeneutics, *Unfamiliar metaphors in Hosea 14:6-7*, (https://hermeneutics.stackexchange.com/questions/1894/unfamiliar-metaphors-in-hosea-146-7 2012)

Mike Bickle, Library Forerunner School of Ministry, *STUDIES IN THE BEAUTY OF GOD – MIKE BICKLE Session 6 Behold a Throne and One Who Sits on It (Rev. 4:2)*, 2006

gotquestions.org, *What does it mean that Zerubbabel was the LORD's signet ring (Haggai 2:23)?* (https://www.gotquestions.org/Zerubbabel-signet-ring.html 2022)

David Guzik, *PSALM 149 – THE HIGH PRAISES OF GOD AND A TWO-EDGED SWORD*, The Enduring Word Bible Commentary,   (https://enduringword.com/bible-commentary/psalm-149 2020)

Pure Life Ministries, *The Fear of the Lord is the Beginning of Wisdom | 20 Truths that Help the Battle with Porn Addiction*, (https://www.youtube.com/watch?v=6BwGOrFKSVw 2019)

E.   Swedenborg,   *Spiritual   Meaning   of   Forehead*, (http://www.biblemeanings.info/Words/Body/Forehead.htm 2002)

thefreedictionary.com,   homage, https://www.thefreedictionary.com/Hommage. American Heritage® Dictionary of the English language, Fifth Edition. Copyright © 2016 by Houghton Mifflin Harcourt Publishing Company. Published by Houghton Mifflin Harcourt Publishing Company. All rights reserved.

Songs

Martin Luther, and Fredrick H. Hedge, *A Mighty Fortress is Our God*,   (https://hymnary.org/text/a_mighty_fortress_is_our_god_a_bulwark, public domain)

Don't miss out!

Visit the website below and you can sign up to receive emails whenever Dennis Grimes publishes a new book. There's no charge and no obligation.

https://books2read.com/r/B-A-KJUCB-IHGWC

BOOKS 2 READ

Connecting independent readers to independent writers.

Also by Dennis Grimes

Generation Zion

Generation Zion

The Melchizedek Priesthood Garments

The Melchizedek Priesthood Robes

About the Author

Dennis Grimes resides in Paris, TX with his wife Faith and two children. He is a Prayer Shepherd. Besides being a Prayer Shepherd, he is an itinerant minister at Teen Blaze/First Youth Nations in Southern California and Believers Ministry International. His passion for prayer and revival is sparked to see a multigenerational movement of God that will help bring forth the Global End-Time Harvest and End-Time Revival.